Editor
Gisela Lee, M.A.

Managing Editor
Karen J. Goldfluss, M.S. Ed.

Editor-in-Chief
Sharon Coan, M.S. Ed.

Cover Art
Brenda DiAntonis

Illustrator
Renée Christine Yates

Art Manager
Kevin Barnes

Art Director
CJae Froshay

Imaging
Rosa C. See

Product Manager
Phil Garcia

Interior Art Concepts
Ann Greenman Barnell

Publishers
Rachelle Cracchiolo, M.S. Ed.
Mary Dupuy Smith, M.S. Ed.

Authors

Jane Carroll Routte and Ann Greenman Barnell

Teacher Created Materials, Inc.
6421 Industry Way
Westminster, CA 92683
www.teachercreated.com
ISBN-0-7439-3719-8
©2004 Teacher Created Materials, Inc.
Made in U.S.A.

Table of Contents

Introduction

Greece is a country with a rich heritage. From the wonders of the ancient Greek civilization to the present day, Greece is full of variety and life. History, science, literature, mathematics, and government all owe much to the Greek thinkers. Food, dance, music, and art have a place in the daily lives of the Greek people. Greece has affected Western Civilization in every area of the arts and sciences throughout time. It is no wonder that Greece is often referred to as the "Cradle of Western Civilization."

The activities in this book will help to introduce students to the widely varied culture and history of Greece. Rich literature is represented through Greek mythology and the timeless stories of Aesop, along with more modern books. The ancient Greeks were the inventors of drama, and students can practice their dramatic skills while doing choral readings. Vocabulary study is enhanced through a look at the roots of English words influenced by the Greek language. Students will have an opportunity to learn to count to 10 in Greek.

Studying the Olympics will give students the chance to practice athletic competitions, get to know more about the history and traditions of the games, and become involved with the upcoming Olympic games. Students can keep score and use their math skills to determine winners in classroom competitions. They can plan their own classroom or school-wide Olympic Games complete with an opening ceremony, lighting of the torch, and crowning of the winners. We recommend that the class Olympics be used as a final activity where the students can display their flags, reports, pictures, and perhaps put on a Greek play, complete with dress and masks.

A taste of Greek food will enhance the learning experience while students examine traditions of the Greek islands and the people who live there. Students can explore the history of worry beads, icons, and other traditions. Activities will lead students to a greater appreciation of the way that people live in this very different country.

Ancient Greece is included in the activities. Students will have a chance to design and wear Greek clothing. They can also design pottery and go on an archeological dig to search for ancient treasure. Math skills are applied as they make and spend ancient coins.

The ancient Greeks shopped in marketplaces called *agoras*. In the agora Greeks shopped for food and daily items, as well as more luxurious and expensive items. The agora provided a place for trade, but also for socializing and interaction. Creating an agora is another good culminating activity for your class. There the students can display the items they have made, wear ancient Greek clothing, trade with old coins, and share their reports and pictures. Students can make items to sell for drachma at the market. You could have the agora as part of the class Olympics so that all children will have a role in the activity.

This book represents a doorway to the world of Greece. During your study of this amazing country, you will find that there are many new things to learn about this ancient land.

Bibliography

Aesop. *Aesop's Fables*. Exeter Books, 1987.

Ancient Greece. JWM Productions. VHS, 1998.

Athens and Ancient Greece. Questar video, 1998.

Coolidge, Olivia. *Greek Myths*. Houghton Mifflin Company, 1949.

D'aulaire, Ingri and Edgar Parin. *Book of Greek Myths*. Doubleday, 1962.

Davis, Kevin. *Look What Came from Greece*. Franklin Watts, 1999.

Dubin, Mark. *The Greek Islands*. Eyewitness Travel Guides, Dorling Kindersley, 1997.

Evslin, Bernard. *The Greek Gods*. Scholastic, Inc., 1984.

Greece: A Moment of Excellence. Time-Life Video and Television, VHS, 1995.

Haskins, Jim and Kathleen Benson. *Count Your Way Through Greece*. Lerner Publishing, 1996.

History Channel Video. *The Rise and Fall of the Spartans*. 2002.

Hollinger, Peggy. *Greece*. Bookright Press, 1989.

Honan, Linda. *Spend a Day in Ancient Greece*. John Wiley and Sons, Inc., 1998.

Knight, Theodore. *The Olympic Games*. Lucent Books, Inc., 1991.

Macdonald, Fiona. *I Wonder Why Greeks Built Temples*. Larousse Kingfisher Chambers, Inc., 1997.

Marani, Anna. *Olympic and Olympic Games*. Toubi's, 1999.

Nam, Yeoh Hong. *Greece (Countries of the World)*. Gareth Stevens Publishing, 1999.

Oxlade, Chris and David Ballheimer. *Olympics*. Fitzgerald, 2001.

Pearson, Anne. *Ancient Greece*. Eyewitness Books, Dorling Kindersley, 2000.

Pearson, Anne. *Everyday Life in Ancient Greece*. Franklin Watts, 1994.

Philip, Neil. *Mythology*. Eyewitness Books, Dorling Kindersley, 2000.

Pinkney, Jerry. *Aesop's Fables*. North-South Books, 2000.

Proddow, Penelope. *Hermes, Lord of Robbers*. Doubleday & Company, Inc., 1971.

Purdy, Susan and Cass R. Sandak. *Ancient Greece*. Franklin Watts, 1999.

Internet Resources

http://www.culture.gr/2/21/218/e21800.html (Greek artwork)

www.gogreece.com

www.in2greece.com

www.explorecrete.com

www.olympic.org (official site of the Olympic movement)

http://www.nineplanets.org/mercury.html (information about the planet Mercury)

http://pds.jpl.nasa.gov/planets/welcome.htm (information about the planets)

http://www.forumancientcoins/forvm/first.html (catalogue of ancient Greek coins)

http://www.eatgreek.com/index.html (online store for Greek food and festival items)

http://www.fathertimes.net/greeknewyear.htm (Greek New Year traditions)

http://mywebpages.comcast.net/dougsmit/ (good site for history of Greek coins)

http://www.kypros.org/cgi-bin/lexicon (Greek translator)

http://www.olympic.org/uk/games/athens/index_uk.asp (Olympic information)

http://www.factmonster.com/ipka/A088/1992.htm (Greek monsters)

http://alumni.imsa.edu/~chuck/project/mask-type.html (information about masks used in Greek tragedy including construction techniques)

http://www.georama.gr/eng/junior/birds/014.html (information about the birds of Greece)

http://www.vic.com/asteria/ (Greek dances; it shows dance steps and pictures of people dancing)

http://abcteach.com (black outline map of Greece for coloring)

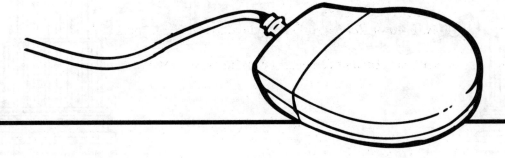

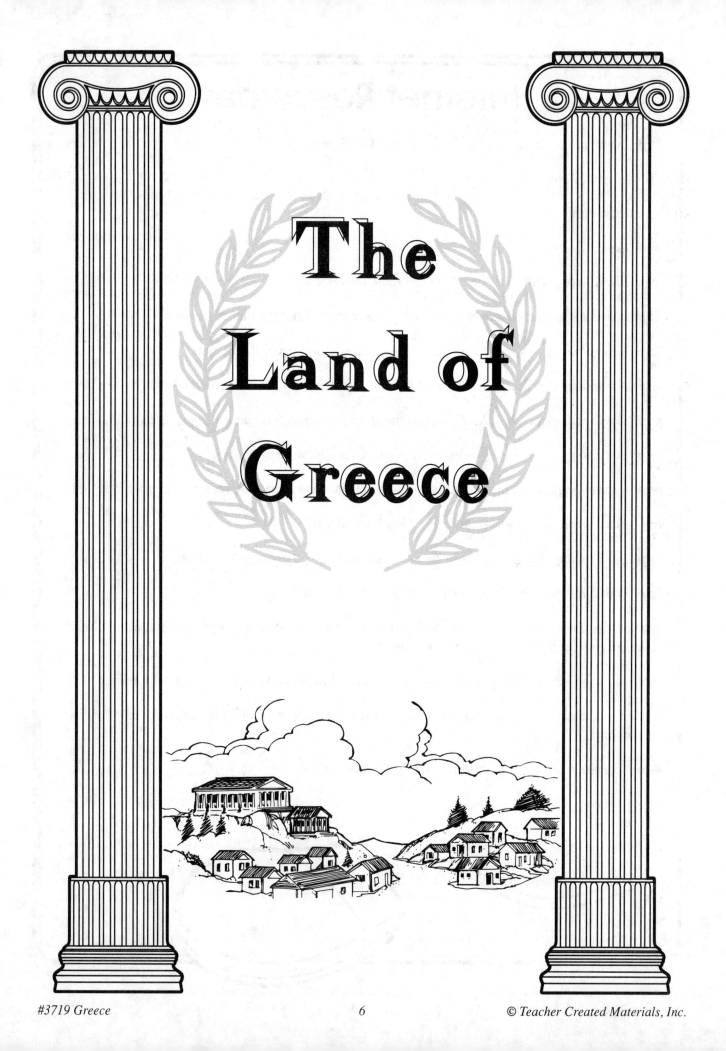

The Land of Greece

Gifts from Greece

Greece is often called the "Cradle of Western Civilization," and for a good reason. Many of the ideas and things that people take for granted today were born in Greece thousands of years ago.

The Greeks were very fond of science, math, and learning. They were the first to organize schools and libraries. They also developed mathematical ideas such as fractions and geometry. They organized much of their knowledge in the first encyclopedias. They were among the first to study the human body and how it works. This science is called *anatomy*.

The Greeks created a system of government in which people could vote for their rulers. They called this government a *democracy*. It is the same way the government of the United States operates today. Many other countries of the world use the same system.

Sports were important to the Greeks. They started the Olympics, boxing, and marathons. They were the first to build stadiums for people to watch athletic events.

Greek people also enjoyed getting together to see plays, and they were the first to put on plays in theaters. Their plays were called *comedies* and *tragedies*. The actors would wear costumes and masks, and they would use special effects to amuse the audiences.

There are many ways people benefit from the knowledge of the Greeks. Can you find out more?

Gifts from Greece Riddles

Here are four riddles about things that came from the Greeks. Can you figure them out?

Riddle #1

Above I name a part.
Below I name the whole.
I'm smaller on the top
Than I am on the bottom.
Because if I were not
Then I'd be improper!

Riddle #2

I am at the heart of the matter.
Some people would give an arm and a leg
To know more about me.
I can save lives and help you be strong.

Riddle #3

People from all over the world
Gather to be part of me.
There are many of me every year
In many cities and countries.
Sometimes I am large and famous.
Sometimes I am small and little known,
But I always have my 26.2 miles (42 km).

Riddle #4

My first part means "people."
My second part means "government."
You can vote for or against me,
Because the choice is yours.

Hint: Fold this section under before reproducing.

Answers: 1. fraction **2.** science anatomy **3.** marathon **4.** democracy

Which of These Words Came from Greek?

Many of the words we use today came from the Greek language. Put an X next to the words that you think came from Greek culture. Then check the next page to see if you were correct.

_____ 1. cleaver	_____ 6. alphabet
_____ 2. gymnasium	_____ 7. bicycle
_____ 3. planet	_____ 8. elephant
_____ 4. dachshund	_____ 9. hippopotamus
_____ 5. rhinoceros	_____ 10. turkey

Hint: Fold this section under before reproducing.

1. cleaver—No. This is a word from Old English. It means a heavy knife or hatchet.

2. gymnasium—Yes. This was the name of the schools where students also learned about sports in ancient Greece.

3. planet—Yes. This word came from *planasthai*, which meant to wander. Planets look like wandering stars.

4. dachshund—No. This word comes from the German language. *Dach* means badger and *hund* means hunt.

5. rhinoceros—Yes. *Rhin* or *rhino* means nose or nasal. *Keros* means horn. A rhinoceros has a large horn on its nose.

6. alphabet—Yes. *Alpha* is the name of the first letter of the Greek alphabet. *Beta* is the name of the second letter.

7. bicycle—Yes. *Bi* means two. *Kylos* means wheel. What do we call a three-wheeled bicycle?

8. elephant—Yes. The Greek word for elephant was *elephas*.

9. hippopotamus—Yes. *Hippos* means horse, and *potamos* means river. Hippopotami are large animals that live mostly in or near rivers. The plural can be either hippopotami or hippopotamuses. Can you spell these words?

10. turkey—No. Turkeys are birds that come from North America. The Greeks would never have seen a turkey.

Which "Polis" Do You Live In?

If you look at a map of the United States, you will see that there are many cities whose names end in "polis." There is Annapolis, Indianapolis, Minneapolis. Do you know of any other ones?

Why do the names of these cities have that ending? Well, that comes from Greece.

Greece is a country of many small islands and a rocky, mountainous mainland. In ancient times, it was difficult for people to travel from place to place. About 1200 B.C., the Greeks began to form city-states. These city-states were small areas of the country that surrounded cities. They would be named for the city that they were built around. For example, the city-state around Athens was named "Athens." The one around the city of Sparta was called "Sparta" and so forth. At one point in time, there were more than 700 city-states in Greece.

The city-states would have their own laws, their own rulers, and their own ways of doing things. This is where the idea of democracy was born. Many of the city-states in Greece allowed the people to vote and have a voice in the government. Eventually, Greece became known as the "Cradle of Democracy."

The Greek name for these city-states was "polis." Now when people speak about cities, people use the ancient Greek term. Any large city is called a *metropolis* (from the Greek *meter*, which means mother, and *polis*, which means city). What do people call a very large urban area that includes many towns and cities close together? A megalopolis! (*Mega* means big.)

Activity

Look at a map of the United States. See how many cities you can find that end in "polis." Have a contest with other students to see who can make the longest list. Be sure to include the name of the state where they are located.

Put a map up in your classroom and stick colorful pins in the names of all the cities that end in "polis."

How the Greeks Help Us Stay Healthy

Have you ever been to see a doctor? Did you know that over 2,000 years ago Greek doctors created many of the practices used by doctors today?

One of the most famous of the Greek doctors was named Hippocrates (460–366 B.C.). Hippocrates was the first doctor to use the method of diagnosis. When doctors diagnose a patient's condition, they look at all of the symptoms and decide on the treatment that is needed. Before Hippocrates came up with this system, treatment was based on superstition. Hippocrates is often called the "Father of Modern Medicine."

Doctors take the "Hippocratic Oath" today. In the oath, they promise to do no harm to their patients. The oath is named for Hippocrates, but he probably did not write it. He did write many papers about medicine and his ideas, but most of them have been lost over the years.

Herophilus was another famous Greek scientist. He studied anatomy. *Anatomy* is the science of understanding the parts of the body and how they work. He gave names to different parts of the body and made a book with drawings of the human body and its parts. Understanding how the body works is important for the doctors of today.

Asclepiades was another important doctor. He thought that wine helped patients recover from illness. He also believed that doctors should have a pleasant bedside manner. Today, doctors realize that this is very important when treating their patients.

Asclepius was the Greek god of medicine. His symbol was a snake wound around a staff. This symbol is still used by doctors today and is called the *caduceus*.

Activity

Find out more about the doctors mentioned here and write a report to share with your class.

A Body of Knowledge

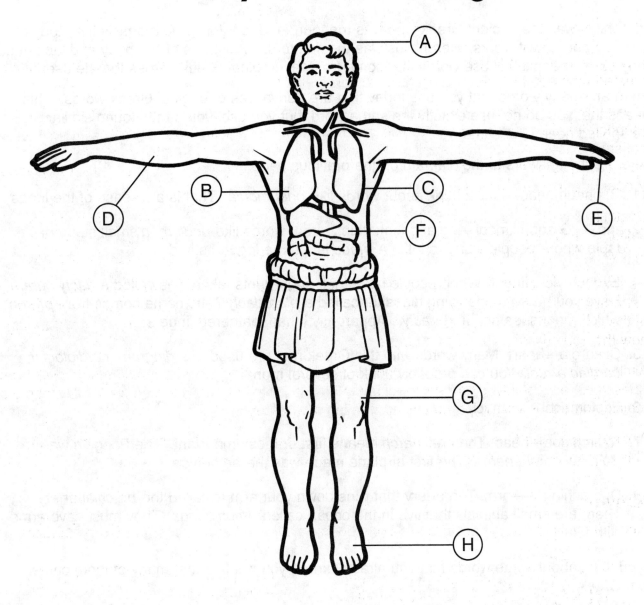

A Greek doctor gave names to many of the parts of the human body. Doctors today still use some names that are similar to the Greek names. Can you match the Greek names for these body parts to the picture above?

1. pneumonas _____

2. podi _____

3. podi _____

4. dachtylo _____

5. kardio _____

6. stomachi _____

7. archigos _____

8. brachionas _____

A Body of Knowledge *(cont.)*

Herophilus was the ancient Greek who was the founder of anatomy. *Anatomy* is the study of the body and how it works. Herophilus was the first to draw pictures of the body and label the body parts. People still use words that come from the original Greek names that he used.

There are many words that you use today that are derivatives of original Greek words. This means that you do not use exactly the same word, but you use words that sound similar or are spelled nearly the same way.

Here are the answers to the diagram on the previous page.

1. B; pneumonas—lungs; think about words like *pneumonia*. That is a disease of the lungs.

2. and 3. G and H; podi—leg and foot; think about words like *podium, a* small stand or table where people stand to talk. A *tripod* is a three-legged stand.

4. E; dachtylo—finger When people have their fingerprints taken, it is called a *dactylogram*. Have you heard of the flying dinosaur called a *pterodactyl*? Its name comes from *pteron*, which means feather, and *dactyl*. Apparently it had feathered fingers!

5. C; kardio—heart Many words with this Greek root are used: *cardiogram, cardiologist, cardiac arrest*. You can probably think of several more.

6. F; stomachi—stomach

7. A; archigos—head The prefix *arch* means first or most important. The Penguin was Batman's *archenemy*. The first airplane made was the *archetype*.

8. D; brachionas—arm The artery that runs down your arm is called the *brachial artery*. There are small animals that live in the ocean called *brachiopods*. They must have arms with feet!

If you think about some words that you already know, you will find that many of them came from Greek.

Map Projects

Maps are good projects to display around the classroom. Three-dimensional maps bring to life the actual physical characteristics of an area. These map projects will help your students visualize the country of Greece and its topography.

Here are two map-making projects which you may choose to use in your classroom:

Use a black outline map of Greece. Project the map onto a large sheet of white paper on a wall for the students to trace. After the outlines of the country are traced, have the students write in the names of the islands. Students may want to color the islands and/or groups of islands in the manner of a political map.

Have the students make a topographical map using a recipe of flour, salt, and water to make a dough mixture. (See recipe below.) Project the map outline on to a large piece of cardboard. Use the dough mixture to form the shapes of the Greek islands. Have students look at topographical maps to add the mountains and plains. This map may take some time to dry properly. Have the students paint the various geographical areas in different colors. Small flags can be glued to toothpicks and stuck into the map to show important cities and places of interest.

Recipe for Dough

Mix one part flour with one part salt.

Gradually stir in water until mixture is thick but not too wet. The mixture should be the consistency of clay, and easily be molded into mountains.

You may add food coloring to the mixture or paint the map after it is dry.

Allow this type of map sufficient time to dry; it may take one or two days depending upon the humidity.

Famous Thinkers Puzzle

Many famous scientists and philosophers came from Greece. See if you can unscramble their names in the spaces below.

1. ____ ____ ____ ____ ____ ____ ____ ____

2. ____ ____ ____ ____ ____

3. ____ ____ p ____ ____ ____ ____ ____ ____ ____ ____

4. A ____ ____ ____ ____ ____ ____ ____ ____ ____ ____

5. ____ ____ ____ ____ ____ ____ ____ ____ ____

6. ____ ____ ____ ____ ____ ____

7. P ____ ____ ____ ____ ____ ____ ____ ____ ____

8. ____ ____ ____ ____ ____ ____ ____ ____

9. ____ ____ ____ ____ ____ m ____ ____ ____ ____

List of Names

otapl	sarogahtyp	ttoilears
chemisdear	dliuec	pocratpihse
sdiecaslpae	shilopuerh	tessorac

- -

Hint: Fold this section under before reproducing. You may want to put the unscrambled names on the board to give extra clues.

Answers: 1. Socrates **2.** Plato **3.** Hippocrates **4.** Asclepiades **5.** Herophilus **6.** Euclid **7.** Pythagoras **8.** Aristotle **9.** Archimedes

A Flag for Greece

Greece is a land of sun and sea. The flag of Greece reflects the beautiful blue that is so much a part of the country.

In the past the country has had two different flags. One was blue and white stripes. The other one had a white cross on a blue background. The flag that Greece uses today is a combination of those two flags. This flag was adopted by Greece on December 22, 1978.

The flag has nine blue and white stripes and a blue field with a white cross in the upper left-hand corner. There are different reasons given for the nine stripes. One story is that there are nine letters in the Greek word for freedom. Another version is that there are nine syllables in the phrase "Eleutheria H Thanatos" which means "Liberty or Death."

The white cross symbolizes the Greek Orthodox faith. Greek Orthodoxy is the official religion of Greece. The color white symbolizes the purity of the Greek fight for freedom from Turkish rule in the nineteenth century. Some say that the white represents the waves of the sea.

On the next page is a flag of Greece to color. The top and bottom stripes are blue. Alternate white with blue to complete the stripes. The field behind the cross is blue.

When you are finished with your flag, display it in your classroom or at home. If you color both sides, it will look like a real flag!

Greek Flag Template

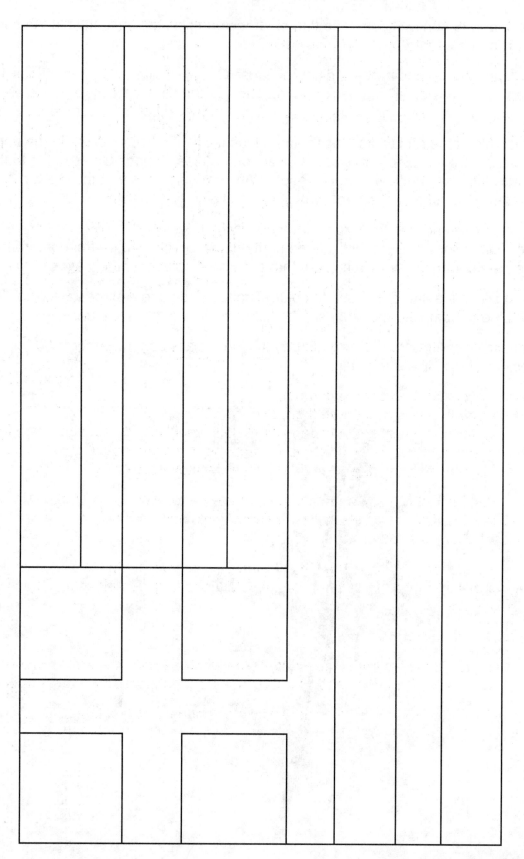

16

Sponges

Have you ever used a sponge to clean something? You probably know that sponges are full of holes and are used for washing cars or cleaning other things around the house. Most of the sponges that you see and use today are man-made. Natural sponges are actually little animals that live in the sea.

Sponges grow on rocks and hard surfaces under the water. They have to be cut away from the rocks and cleaned before they can be used by us. Sponge divers have to go very deep under the water to harvest sponges.

The Greek island of Kalymnous is famous for its sponge farming. For many hundreds of years, divers have cut the sponges from the rocks around this island. There are pictures of sponge divers on pottery that is more than 500 years old.

Diving for sponges can be very dangerous. Divers used to carry heavy rocks with them to help them sink to the bottom of the ocean where they would cut the sponges from the rocks. When they collected the sponges, they would drop the rocks and rise back up to the surface of the water. Sometimes the divers would drown while they were doing their jobs.

Before the boats go out to search for sponges, there is a festival called "Ipogros "or "Sponge Week Festival." The islanders celebrate with food, drink, and dancing. The people dress in traditional costumes for the festivities.

When Greek immigrants came to the United States, they often settled in areas where they could work at their old jobs. In Tarpon Springs, Florida, a large Greek settlement still keeps the old traditions of sponge harvesting.

Activities

Scientists used to classify sponges as plants. Later, they decided that sponges are more like animals. Find out about sponges and how they are like plants and how they are like animals.

Find pictures of different types of sponges. Make a sponge scrapbook and tell about the different types of sponges you discovered.

Sponges Are for More Than Just Cleaning!

You probably think of a sponge as something to clean with, but have you ever thought of using a sponge as a paintbrush?

People use sponges to apply paint to walls and furniture. Sponges make unusual patterns because of their interesting and different surfaces. You can use sponges to paint walls and furniture. You can decorate boxes or just about anything that you can think of.

Try this painting project to practice the sponge painting technique:

Materials

- acrylic or tempera paint
- sponges (natural or synthetic)
- paper
- stencils

Directions

1. Place a small amount of paint on a flat surface such as a plate.

2. Dab the sponge in the paint.

3. Practice on a sheet of newspaper to get the effect that you want and to take off excess paint.

4. Secure the stencil to the working surface with tape or hold firmly with your hand.

5. Lightly dab paint onto stencil areas that you want to paint.

6. To mix colors, put the second color on another sponge and add on top.

7. Carefully remove stencil and let dry.

8. Optional: To make the stencils, trace the stencil design by pushing with a ball point pen onto tag board or poster board. Use a small utility knife to cut out stencils.

Saving the Loggerhead Sea Turtle on Zakinthos

Tourists come every year to experience the natural beauty of the Greek Islands. Since Greece depends on the sea for food and cherishes its beauty, keeping the water clean is important to its people.

The word *ecology* comes from the Greek word "oikos" which means "house." Keeping one's environmental house in order is an important part of a good ecosystem.

The loggerhead sea turtles that live near Zakinthos are now an endangered species. People hunted them for their meat and shells. A conservation project to protect egg-laying sites for these rare turtles (only 800 remained in 1997) is underway in Laganas. Goals are to protect the eggs from poachers and to keep the oceans free of pollution.

The turtles can weigh up to 400 pounds (180 kilograms) each. These turtles have been migrating from Africa to the Greek islands to lay their eggs at night in the soft Greek sand for thousands of years. Now, their homes are disturbed by the presence of people.

Not only are the loggerhead turtles rare but so are the Greek turtle coins from the mountainous island of Aegina. These coins are prized because some believe them to be the world's first coins. They were made of a mixture of gold and silver and stamped with the sea turtle.

Project "Jago," a small submarine, has gotten marine biologists involved along the almost 9,500 miles (15,289 km) of Greek coastline. Not only have they discovered new types of fish, but they are also helping Greece replenish its fishing grounds.

Marnix Hoekstra volunteers for the Archelon Sea Turtle Protection Society of Greece every summer. This society helps turtles that have been hit by boats, have been captured in nets, have oil or tar on their bodies, or have diseases. On his Website you can see where the turtles lay their eggs. These places include Falari, Marathonis, Crete, Zakynthos, and others. Go to:

www.geocities.com/mfhoekstra/Turtles.html or www.seaturtle.org.

Another site features the Kefalonian Marine Turtle Project in the Ionian Sea. The island is described as the greenest of the islands due to the fir trees that grow there. It is also lush with olive trees, lemon trees, and grapevines. This island has a long coastline of 158 miles (254 km). The turtle project which started in 1984 was to monitor the population of the loggerhead turtles on the island. The nesting area on the southeast tip of the island is almost 2.8 miles (4.5 km), and students who are interested in biology come to help with the project. They estimate that there are about 2,000 to 4,000 of this type of turtle left in the Mediterranean Sea.

The Greek dilemma is: turtles or tourists? Tourism is the largest industry, and tourists outnumber the local inhabitants during certain seasons. It is also during the July–August season that the turtles want to incubate their eggs. Environmental groups fight to preserve the nesting grounds while developers want the land for the tourists. The noise and lights keep the mother turtles from coming to the beach, and the eggs are dropped in the ocean. Some turtles choke on plastic bags which they think are jelly fish, their favorite food. The turtles and eggs are hit by boats and the eggs are pierced by beach umbrellas.

How would you solve this problem?

Read the poem "Turtles and Me" on Marnix Hoekstra's Website. It was written by a young man interested in saving the turtles. What type of poem can you write about saving endangered species?

Create a Sea Turtle or "Jago" Picture

Materials

- white glossy paper
- crayons and blue paint, brushes, or sponges

Directions

1. Using your crayons draw a turtle swimming in the ocean surrounded by vegetation or draw a picture of the Jago searching for sea life.

2. Paint over the crayon with the blue paint using a brush or sponge to give the effect of the ocean.

3. Write a poem and attach it to your picture.

Turtles brown and green should always be seen! Save the Sea Turtles!!

Greece has other endangered species you might want to investigate and write about.

The Imperial Eagle is very rare in Europe. It nests in Greece during the winter months, and its numbers are decreasing every year.

You can also find out about the endangered Audouin's Gull. This is a seabird that was in danger of extinction, but now its numbers are increasing. Find out how these birds have been helped.

What other endangered species can you learn about?

Making a Turtle Stamp or Other Endangered Species Coins

Materials

- oven-bake modeling clay
- plastic knives, ceramic tools, or pencils
- acrylic paints
- *optional:* cookie dough

Directions

1. You will need a small clump of clay the size of an egg.

2. Form the clay in your hand so that it fits between your thumb and finger.

3. Work the clay to form a small oval.

4. Using plastic knives, ceramic tools, or pencils, carve the shape of a turtle or any other symbol.

5. Let dry completely and then bake in oven as instructed on directions given on clay packaging.

6. To create uniform coins, the Greeks pushed a die (stamp) into hot metal. Use the stamp as the Greeks did to make their coins alike. Push it into small balls of one-inch clay that will end up being about ½-inch (1.2 cm) thick. (Almost like making a peanut butter cookie!)

7. Draw and fire the new coins.

8. Paint or glaze the coins and use them for your market day or display.

9. Another variation would be to use any kind of plain cookie dough. The stamp (once cleaned) can make the same impression before baking. The class may want to have cookies representing different currency and use them in their market place for trading.

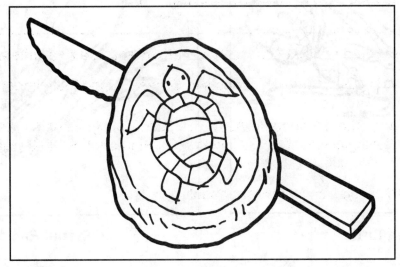

Endangered Species

Audouin's Gull

Sea Turtle

Brown Bear

Imperial Eagle

Santorini – An Island with a Secret

One Greek island with an interesting history is Santorini. Today, Santorini is a beautiful crescent-shaped island with whitewashed buildings in the bright Greek sunshine. But Santorini was not always like this. In fact, much of the island disappeared when a volcano erupted about 3,500 years ago.

Santorini used to be a round island. In 1500 B.C. a large volcano on the island erupted. The eruption caused the center of the island to disappear beneath the ocean. The people who lived on the island knew that the volcano was going to erupt, and they left the island. No one is certain where they went. Some people think they might have gone to Egypt. There are clues that the Greek culture was taken to Egypt about that time.

Today, many tourists visit Santorini to see the archaeological remains of the town of Akrotiri. When the people left Akrotiri, they left it in a hurry. The town is very much like it was before the volcano. The walls of the buildings are only half-high, but the archaeologists can tell what the houses looked like and much about how the people lived.

Many of the colorful frescos were taken away from the city. They were put into a museum in Athens. Now they are being brought back. Jars and other remains are in the town to let us know more about how the people lived in those days. Tourists can walk the same streets that the people did 3,500 years ago.

One interesting theory about Santorini is that it may be Atlantis. Atlantis is a mysterious place that was talked about by Plato, a Greek philosopher. He said that Atlantis was an island country that was very advanced. He said that Atlantis had wonderful art and science. He also said that Atlantis disappeared beneath the ocean. No one has ever known whether Atlantis was a reality or a myth. Maybe the secret will be found in Santorini.

Activities

Although Santorini was destroyed by a volcano, many islands are formed by volcanoes that come up from the bottom of the ocean. Many of the Greek islands, the Hawaiian Islands, Japan, and other islands in the world were formed this way. Many of these islands still have active volcanoes on them. Do some research about volcanoes and see how many islands you can learn about that were formed by volcanoes.

Here are the names of some famous volcanoes that have erupted. Look up these volcanoes and report on what you discover.

Mt. Pelee – 1902	Mt. Saint Helens – 1980	Lake Nyos – 1986
Nevado del Ruiz – 1985	Paricutin – 1943	Krakatau – 1883

A Summary of the Greek Islands

Greece is a country made up of over 3,000 islands. Some of the islands are very large, some are very small. The islands are divided into groups. Here is a list of some of the more important islands in Greece.

Crete—The largest island. Crete was the home of the Minoan civilization, and today the palace of Knossos is an important achaeological site.

The Cyclades Islands—This group includes 220 islands. This group of islands was formed by volcanic action. The main islands and some interesting facts about them are:

Andros—Very mountainous with well-watered valleys. This island has an ancient temple to Dionysus.

Delos—This island is currently uninhabited, but it contains many important sites for archaeology. In ancient times it was an important political center.

Ios—This island is only 11 miles (18 km) long and 6 miles (9.6 km) wide. Only about 1,200 people live there. It is very popular with young tourists.

Milos—Has hot sulphur springs and exports salt and gypsum. Many beautiful works of ancient art have been discovered here, including the *Venus de Milo* in the Louvre Museum of Paris.

Naxos—This is the largest and most fertile of the Cyclades group. This island also has beautiful beaches. Mount Zas is the highest mountain in the Aegean Sea. There are many ancient ruins here.

Paros—This island gets its wealth from exporting parian marble, a very fine and translucent white marble. The island has a good port for ships. There are also remains of a medievel castle and a monastery.

Santorini (also called Thira)—This island is famous for being the spot of an ancient volcanic eruption that caused widespread destruction in the Mediterranean area.

Other islands in this group include: Kea, Kithnos, Serifos, Syros (Siros, Syra), Mykonos, and Tinos.

The Dodecanese Islands—These islands are far from the mainland of Greece and close to the coast of Turkey. Their main income is from tourism, with some fishing, grapes, and olives.

Pátmos—This island is famous for being the island where John wrote the "Book of Revelations" in the *Bible*.

Rhodes—This island has been very important in the history of the world. Many battles and important military happenings occurred on Rhodes. The "Colossus of Rhodes," a giant statue to the sun god Helios, was erected on this island and was one of the Seven Wonders of the Ancient World.

Other islands in this group include Astipálaia, Kálimnos, Kárpathos, Kásos, Kastellórizo, Khalki, Kós, Léros, Nisiros, Simi, Tilos, and Samos

A Summary of the Greek Islands *(cont.)*

The Sporades Islands—These islands are in the Aegean Sea near the coast of Turkey.

  Lesvos—This island is mentioned in the *Odyssey* by Homer and was one of the stops made in the journey home from Troy. Olives and grapes grow on this island.

  Other islands in this group are Limnos and Khios.

The Ionian Islands—These islands are off the west coast of the Greek mainland in the Ionian Sea. Grapes, olives, fishing, and tourism are important to these islands.

  Corfu—This island is often considered to be one of the most beautiful of the Greek islands. It is famous for its olive trees and olive production.

  Ithaki—This island was mentioned in Homer's *Odyssey,* but it was called Ithaca.

  Kefalonia—This is the largest of the Ionian Islands. This island is also the setting for *Captain Corelli's Mandolin*, a love story about World War II in Greece. This island has beautiful beaches and lush vegetation.

  Lefkada—This island is connected to the mainland with a causeway.

  Zakynthos—The inhabitants of this island are working hard to preserve the sea turtles which use their beaches for laying eggs.

  Another island in this group is Paxi.

Saronic Islands—These small islands are in the Saronic Gulf near the mainland of Greece.

  Aegina—This island's largest crop is pistachio nuts. Other crops are cotton, almonds, and figs. Sponge fishing is also important here. This island has many important archaeological sites.

  Hydra—No motor vehicles are allowed on this island, so all transportation is provided by donkey taxies.

  Other islands in this group are Poros and Spetses.

Activities

Divide the class into groups and have them do research on an individual island or groups of islands. They can locate the islands on maps and tell a little about each one.

Have the students draw maps of their islands. Make a classroom atlas of the Greek islands by collecting all of the maps.

Have the students research traditions, food, music, or dancing that is particular to their islands. Because Greece is comprised of so many small islands, there are traditions on some islands that are not popular in other parts of the country.

Discuss with students the difficulty of having a country that is separated by water. Discuss with them how that difficulty would have been much greater in the past.

How has modern technology made it easier for the people of Greece to get to know each other? How have transportation, television, radio, and computers affected the country? What other modern devices would help with this?

People and Lifestyles

Weaving and Spinning

In Greek society women of all classes created textiles for their households. They could show off their skill and creativity by weaving artistic pieces for their homes. All the clothing for the family was made by hand, and it was an important task. To make fabric the women had to process wool from their sheep or flax from their fields to make linen. They had to clean it, comb it, spin it, dye it, and weave it. Then they could cut the pieces for their garments.

How do you get your clothing today?

Has anyone ever made something for you to wear?

How did they get the material to make it?

Do you think people had a lot of clothing in early Greece? Why or why not?

Women had many jobs to do during their busy day. Some had to tend to their herds of sheep; others gathered food or went to the market. A woman could carry a distaff in her hand, and while she walked, she could spin the wool or flax into thread.

Here is a picture of Penelope's loom, which was drawn on an early Grecian vase. It tells us that the Greeks used vertical looms (the loom is standing straight up).

The threads were woven in and out of the threads on the loom. The threads on the loom are called the "warp threads" and the ones you weave across are called "the woof." You can try weaving with the paper weaving project on page 29.

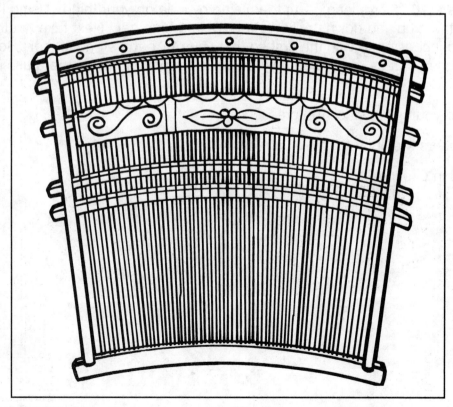

Weaving and Spinning *(cont.)*

Spinning was essential to the ancient Greeks. They had to spin the thread before they could weave it. Most of the cloth made by the Greeks was woven from linen or wool thread.

In order to spin linen or wool fibers into thread, the spinners had to follow a three-step procedure. First, they had to prepare the linen or wool by cleaning and washing it. The fibers had to be straightened before they could be spun. In order to straighten the fibers, the spinner would use an *epinetron*. The epinetron was made of pottery and looked like half of a vase. It fit over the knee of the worker and gave her a surface for teasing the wool or linen into long fibers. After this, the fibers were ready for spinning.

The tool used to spin was called a *spindle*. The spindle was a weight, which pulled down on the fibers and turned, making the fibers twist together into thread. The spinner would hold the wool at the top on a long stick called a *distaff* and let out little bits at a time to keep the thread even. When the threads reached almost to the floor, she would wind up the thread on the spindle and continue the process.

If you would like to try spinning in this manner, you will need to make a spindle. You'll need a pencil and a small potato. Push the pencil through the potato so that the point comes out the other end. Take some fiber (like pillow stuffing) and tie or tape one end to your spindle. Gently spin the potato and watch the fibers twist together. When all of the fibers are twisted, gently pull some more from the stuffing and twist that. It takes some practice to get an even twist. Imagine how long it would take you to spin enough thread to be able to weave a piece of clothing.

Here is another way to understand how spinning works. Take five to seven long grass blades (at least 6 inches (16.25 cm) long). Put them side by side on your thigh. Using the palm of your hand, roll them up and down until they are twisted together. Next take another bunch and overlap two inches or so with the first so that you make the string longer. Soon you will have a short piece of grass rope. See how the twisting motion makes the grass into a stronger rope?

What else could you use besides the grass?

What kinds of fibers are spun to make your clothing?

What was used in Greece?

Woven Placemats

This activity gives students the opportunity to learn the basics of weaving.

Materials (per mat)

- one 18" x 12" (46 cm x 30.5 cm) sheet of construction paper (background color)
- 16 strips of construction paper 1" x 2" (2.54 cm x 5 cm) (accent color)
- scissors
- glue
- ruler
- pencil

Directions

1. Fold the large sheet of paper in half widthwise.

2. Lay a ruler along the folded edge and mark the paper at each inch mark. Do the same along the opposite (open) edge.

3. Measure 1" (2.54 cm) up from the open edge and draw a line across.

4. Draw straight lines from the fold marks to the edge marks.

5. Starting at the folded edge and cutting through both layers, cut along the lines. Be careful to stop 1" from the edge of the paper. This edge holds your loom together.

6. Unfold the paper. This is your "loom."

7. Weave the 1" (2.54 cm) strips through the loom.

8. Glue the ends of the strips to the edges of the loom.

An easy way to make the 1" (2.54 cm) strips is to fold a piece of 9" x 12" (23 cm x 30.5 cm) construction paper lengthwise. Mark every inch along the open and the folded edges. Join the marks with straight lines. Cut along the lines all the way across the paper.

Allow students to experiment with color combinations. Let students try cutting the "loom" with wavy lines for an interesting optical effect.

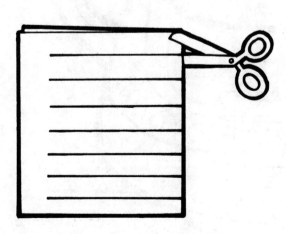

Grecian Oil Lamps

All over the Mediterranean area, for thousands of years, the oil lamp was used like we use a flashlight today since it was small and easy to hold in the hand. These small lamps would also be used in areas where a small amount of light was needed.

You can make your own lamp with a handle, a place to pour in the oil, and an opening for the wick. Original wicks were made from a local plant fiber. You can buy wicks and lamp oil at a store where they sell glass oil lamps. Check your local hardware, craft, or camp stores for availability.

You will need to order a pound of clay per student and have access to a kiln for firing the lamps. Other supplies include a newspaper to work on, plastic bags that seal, a pencil, a plastic knife, and scissors.

Directions

1. Have a student select a pattern and cut out the pattern.
2. Use a wooden rolling pin to roll out the clay to about a ½-inch (1.2-cm) thickness.
3. Trace around the pattern with the pencil pressing it into the clay.
4. Use a plastic knife or the pencil to cut it out.
5. Shape the bottom into the palm of your hand turning up the edges.
6. Set it down to dry a bit until it will stand on its own.
7. Cut the second pattern and form the top shape to your liking.
8. Take the plastic knife and score the edges so that they are rough.
9. Make some slip (a mixture of clay and water) for the mortar to stick the two pieces together.
10. Score the second piece.

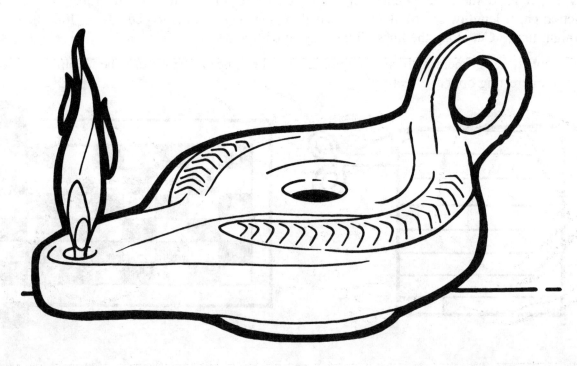

Grecian Oil Lamps *(cont.)*

Direction *(cont.)*

11. Use your fingers, the knife, or a pencil to work the two pieces into a pleasing form.

12. Make a hole in the front with the pencil.

13. Roll a small piece of clay into a 3" to 4" (7.6 cm to 10 cm) coil.

14. Cut the ends.

15. Score them.

16. Score the back of the lamp to attach the handle.

17. Put the slip on the handle and attach.

18. Smooth and decorate the piece using kitchen tools, toothpicks, or the pencil by gently pressing a simple design on the sides, being careful not to collapse the top.

If the clay doesn't work well because it is too dry, just roll it out again and spray it with a little water.

If the clay dries out completely, add a little more water into the bag and form a ball using more water. Then put it into the plastic sack to rework another day.

If students don't have at least 45 minutes to work on this project, have plastic bags ready so that they can store the projects until the next class. The pieces can be assembled at any time.

When the lamps are finished, they should slowly air dry until they are ready for firing.

After the first firing, a stain can be applied for a finish, or a glaze can be applied and then fired again according to the suggested temperature for a shiny finish. Your school art teacher will be able to help you with ordering materials.

Grecian Oil Lamp *(cont.)*

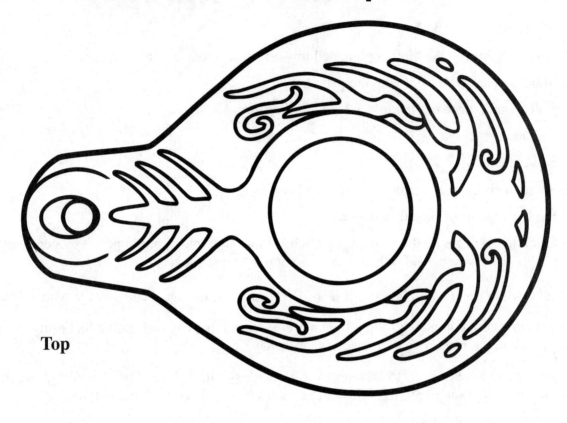

Top

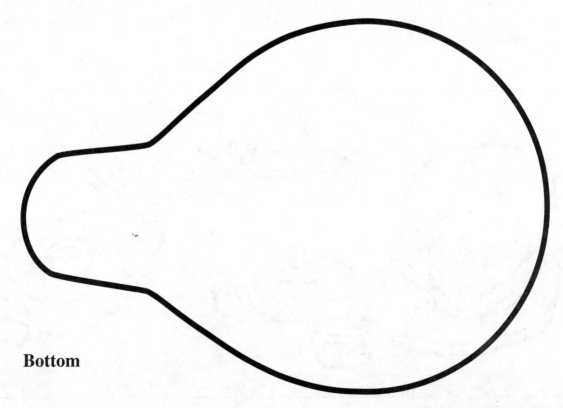

Bottom

Papyrus – Paper from Reeds

When the Greeks occupied Egypt over 2,500 years ago, they learned many important things, but one of the most important was the making of paper from the tall reeds that grew along the Nile River. The best quality paper was made from the inner ring of the reed.

Most of the papyrus manuscripts were written in Greek after Alexander the Great conquered Egypt. Our word *paper* comes from "papyrus" which means "belonging to the house."

Can you imagine what other items could be made from the reeds?

Baskets, boxes, mats, sandals, books, and sails were made from reeds. Even small boats were made from bundles of reeds woven tightly together.

What is most of our paper made from? Most of our paper is made from wood pulp from trees. The technique of making paper from plants continues to this day. In Japan, traditional papers are made from rice. Explore other cultures and find out how they make paper.

It is fun to make your own paper. Handmade paper will be rougher than the paper that you are used to, but people use it to make greeting cards, small wall hangings, special note paper and small pictures.

Materials

- white facial tissues or paper towels
- a screen
- water
- a cookie sheet
- a drying table

Directions

1. Tear the tissues into small pieces.
2. Let the small tissue pieces soak in a small amount of water until the fibers come apart.
3. Place the fibers on the flat screen to drain off the excess water. Press into a flat shape, and place it on the cookie sheet to dry.
4. If you want to make a little scroll, roll the paper to form a scroll and tie it with a ribbon.

Have you ever seen reeds growing along side a river or pond? They are similar to the papyrus reeds of Egypt. Try making paper from them by following these steps.

1. Cut the reeds into the longest strips possible.
2. Weave them together into a small mat.
3. Pound the woven mat with a rock or some tool that won't tear the reeds.
4. Turn it over and pound the other side.
5. Let it dry on a clothes line until it is brown.

The task or making paper was probably done by the house slaves in Egypt and Greece.

A Different Type of Library

What if your books were round instead of square? What if instead of closing your book, you rolled it up? That's what books were like for the ancient Greeks. Books that roll up are called scrolls.

A scroll is really just one long piece of paper. The ends are attached to sticks, and the paper rolls around the sticks to store the scroll. To read a scroll, you only have to unroll the part of the scroll that you are reading. After you read a section, you roll it up and unroll the next part. When you are finished, you have the book all rolled up and ready to put away. Scrolls were usually fastened with strings or ribbons to keep them closed.

It would be fun for you to try making a scroll. You can write a story or a play. You could even do a comic strip on a scroll!

Materials

- five or more sheets of 8½" x 11" (21.5 cm x 28 cm) white paper (Unlined is best because you are going to use it lengthwise.)
- two empty cardboard tubes from aluminum foil or paper towels
- clear tape

Directions

1. Tape the sheets of paper together to make one long piece 8½" (21.5 cm) wide.

2. Tape the ends of the long paper to the empty tubes.

3. Write your story or draw your pictures on the paper between the tubes. Start at one end and write across to the other end.

4. Roll up your scroll and have a friend read it.

5. Put a pretty ribbon around your scroll to keep it closed and to mark it as your own. You can decorate the ends of the tubes that are not covered with the paper. Use decorations that go with your story!

Greek Shadow Puppets

One type of entertainment in Greece is the *karaghiozis* (kah-RAH-gheeoh-zis). These are shadow puppets. The people using the puppets stand behind a screen with light behind them. They put the puppets up near the screen so that the shadow of the puppet shows to the audience. The puppeteers act out familiar stories and tales for the audience.

The influence for the Greek shadow puppets comes form China and India and came to Greece during the Turkish rule. In the Turkish language *kara* means black and *ghioz* means eye. Some say it is named for a Turkish blacksmith who made the sultan angry.

Karaghiozis survives as an example of folk art. It not only entertains but also teaches its audience the history and religion of the Greek people.

The stories may be about everyday life or may include a tale about Alexander the Great or the Greek Revolution of 1821. After World War II it became a show for children rather than families, but its influence has continued to be great. Famous composers like Manos Hatzidakis and Nikos Mamagakis and artist Yiannis Tsarouhis are examples of people who were influenced by the puppet shows.

The characters enter the screen in an order depending upon their wealth. The poor Greeks come out of the shack on the left and the Turks enter from the right from a beautiful palace.

Every character has his or her own music when entering the screen. The music used to be performed live by a group of musicians, but now it is usually done with recordings. The voices may all be done by one person.

Folk artist Costas Makris has shared his designs at this Website:

www.karaghiozis.net/shedia/makris_shediae.html

This site has puppet patterns that you can copy and use to make your own puppets. They also inspire others to create their own characters and stories.

The puppets are created from various body parts (arms, legs, heads, torsos, etc.) that are joined with moving joints that allow them to dance and move like real people. The talented puppeteer can make the shadows seem almost lifelike in the presentations.

You can make a shadow puppet of your own by using the pattern on the next page. Copy the pattern onto heavier paper such as tagboard or poster board. Decorate your character and cut it out. Join the arms, legs, head, and torso at the joints with brads.

Use your puppet to act out a scene from Aesop or Greek mythology. You can create and write your own play and act it out with your classmates and their puppets. Try using your puppets behind a screen of white paper with a light behind them to get the effect of the karaghiozis.

Greek Shadow Puppets *(cont.)*

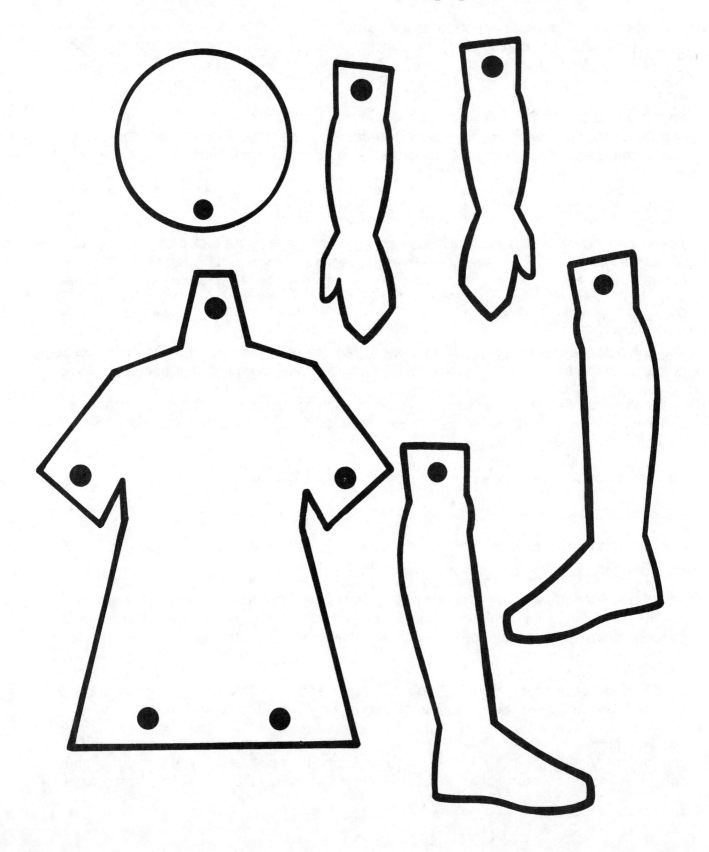

The Evil Eye and Other Superstitions

What causes bad things to happen to people?

Many cultures believe in the "evil eye." The idea has been passed down through many centuries. Whenever something breaks or someone becomes ill, some people think that it is caused by an unknown force. Some believe in the idea that bad luck is caused by an evil spirit's look. Other people find humor in these superstitious beliefs.

Fishermen in Greece sometimes protect their boats by painting eyes on the bows so that monsters and evil forces will stay away. Since fishing is important to the Greeks, they may feel better by having the eyes for protection.

Wearing a necklace of blue beads or pins that look like an eye is another way to find protection. Many adults in Greece wear the beads on their crucifix chains.

Children and adults sometimes wear pilactos. (See page 38.) These are pinned on the outside or inside of clothing to protect the wearer from evil.

Some Greeks believe that if you receive a curse from someone, you can always visit a woman who is old and wise. She will recite biblical passages to end the curse. Those who have seen the results say the curse or illness disappears with no logical scientific explanation.

It was also believed that if someone gave too much praise to something precious, then the evil spirits would try their best to bring misfortune. Therefore, families were slow to praise a newborn child for fear of a curse being placed on the child.

What superstitions do we have about items that protect us? What is the superstition about a rabbit's foot? Why do people like to find four-leaf clovers?

If someone gave you an evil-eye necklace or pilacto, what would you do?

What are superstitions?

Can you name some common superstitions that we have in this country?

Do you believe in any superstitions?

How are superstitions passed down like other traditions?

What do you think of these ideas?

Things to think and write about:

- People often wear necklaces or other jewelry with saints on them. What are some of the saints that people choose? Why?

- On Halloween people wear masks and costumes. This is a very old tradition. Find out where it began and why.

- Sometimes people throw salt over their shoulder if they spill it. Some people never walk under ladders or open umbrellas indoors. Find out how these practices began. Explore other superstitions of this type.

Pilactos

Pilactos are little good-luck charms that some Greek people carry with them. They are little fabric packages that contain herbs and a blessing from the priest. People pin the pilactos to the inside of their clothing to keep them safe from harm.

Pilactos are easy to make and they are nice little gifts to give to a friend or family member.

Materials

- 2½" (6.3 cm) braid or trim about 1" (2.54 cm) wide. You should choose a decorative trim from a fabric store. A nice kind to get is braid with gold thread in it. Good color combinations are red and gold or yellow and gold but anything that you like will work.

- 1 teaspoon of potpourri or other dried herbs. Mint is nice to make a little sachet. Other pleasant smelling herbs are lavender, rosemary, or lemon mint.

- a needle and thread or a sewing machine

- a small gold safety pin

Directions

1. Fold under ¼" (0.6 cm) on each end of the braid.

2. Sew along the finished edges to make a little pouch.

3. Stuff the pouch with the potpourri or dried herbs.

4. Sew up the remaining edge to close.

5. Attach the little safety pin, then pin the pilacto to your clothing or give it away to a friend.

Extra! Extra! Read All About It!

Making a class newspaper is a good way to involve all students in some aspect of learning about Greece. It will also enhance and develop writing and research skills and class participation.

The students will create a newspaper that represents one day in Greece. They may decide to read what happens during a day in Ancient Greece or modern Greece. They may select any time period that your classroom is studying. You may consider doing a newspaper in Athens for the first day of the Olympic games.

Give your students copies of local newspapers to examine. Have the class make a list of different types of items that are found in the newspaper. They will want to include current news, sports, human interest stories, editorials, entertainment, want ads and other advertising, travel, fashion, food, and other items commonly found in newspapers.

Have students take a look at the physical makeup of the newspaper. Talk to them about the use of columns and headlines. Look at the way that newspapers balance the columns, headlines and pictures. Ask students about the arrangement of the newspaper's stories. What goes on the front page? Why? How are other pages organized?

Discuss with the class the jobs that go into publishing a newspaper. Who is going to write news? Who is going to write about fashion? Who is going to plan the newspaper's layout? Who is going to do the artwork?

Many desktop publishing programs have layout templates that will automatically put the newspaper into column format. Once your students decide on the content of the paper, their writing can be put into the program and formatted automatically.

Extra! Extra! Read All About It! *(cont.)*

Once the students decide who is going to write what for the paper, they will need to research their choices in order to begin writing. Students who are doing the fashion writing will have to know about the time period, what was fashionable, and they will have to put it into a newspaper story format.

Here is an example of a feature article that you might use with your class:

> The tunic is all the rage in Greece's fashion world this year. Above the knee is the look this summer. Be sure to have your tunic in the brightest colors. Gold and yellow are the new hot looks. Make a fashion statement by adding one of the latest gold coin belts and matching accessories. Don't forget to add a snake bracelet just above the elbow.

Similar articles can be used with news, sports, and other areas of interest.

Students can do biographical research for a "Man/Woman of the Year" column. They can write ads for selling houses after researching the common look for a Greek home. They might want to sell the Parthenon.

This exercise will also require that the students use their imaginations to add details to their stories. They may write a feature about what it is like to attend school in Greece or maybe what it is like to be a seven-year-old in the Spartan army.

If you are using a desktop publisher, you will be able to import clip art for your pictures. If you cannot import the clip art, then you can add pictures to the final draft before copying.

Teacher's Note: If you are interested in using pictures from the Internet in your paper, you can choose the picture you want, right click on the mouse, and select "copy." Go back to the document that you are working on and select "edit," then "paste." The picture will be pasted into your document. This is a very handy way to acquire pictures for your classroom. Be certain that you are not using the pictures for profit, or you may be in violation of copyright laws.

Extra! Extra! Read All About It! *(cont.)*

Writing a News Story

Teaching students how to write a news story is a good tool for teaching one type of writing organization.

A news story uses "who, what, when, where, why, and how" in order to include all of the necessary information when presenting the news. Students should learn how to ask the right questions, take notes for the answers, and to put the information together in a good, concise way.

As a reporter for the class newspaper, a student may be assigned to cover the winner of the discus throw in the Olympics. The student would have to investigate to learn the following:

> **Who?** Who was the winner of this event?
> Where is he or she from?
>
> **What?** What did they do to win this event?
> What was his or her score?
>
> **When?** When did the event occur?
>
> **Where?** Where was the event held?
>
> **Why/How?** How did they train? How did they learn about the sport? Why does he or she compete?

The students can put together the information that they gather and write the story. A news story is just about the facts. It is usually fairly short and to the point.

A feature story is more of a human interest story that will include information of a more personal nature. A feature may also add opinions and feelings. It will also use the "who, what, when, where, why, and how" method, but the questions may not always be answered at the beginning of a feature.

Use the outline on the following page to help your students learn about writing a good news story.

Extra! Extra! Read All About It! *(cont.)*

Just the Facts

Use this page to gather information for the story that you are going to write for the class newspaper. You can gather your information from books, people, magazines, newspapers, or the Internet.

My topic is _____

Who? Who or what am I writing about?

What? What is important about this?

When? What are the important dates and times for this?

Where? Where are the important places?

Why? Why is this important? Why did it happen?

How? How did this happen? How was it done?

Now put your information together in a good news story that your classmates will enjoy reading.

Making Your Own Worry Beads

Students can be creative in the selection of colors and design of the beads in stringing worry beads. It is important to have beads that won't break easily and will clack when moved.

The pattern on the next page has ¼-inch (0.6 cm) beads, but larger beads may be easier for small hands. It requires blue and yellow plastic beads with a special glass eye bead for protection at the bottom. It uses one small chain with four tiny silver beads at the bottom (see illustration on the next page). Worry beads are also easy to purchase from Websites online for a range of prices.

Directions

1. Buy 20 square beads (or pony beads) in one color, round beads in another, four tiny beads, and one unique bead from a hobby store. Make sure they have large enough holes.

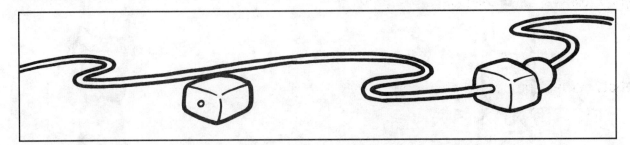

2. In place of the chains, use embroidery floss (undivided), heavy nylon thread, or even satin cord. The size will depend on the size of the beads that you choose. The beads should be able to slide easily on the cord. The string should be 19"–20" (48 cm–51 cm) in length.

3. String 25 beads to match the pattern on the next page. Leave about 3" (7.6 cm) of string on either end of the beads and tie the strings together with a knot. There should be about 2½" (6.35 cm) of string on the other side of the knot. Put both ends through a small bead, the special bead and another small bead and knot again to hold those beads in place. Finish with two beads at the ends of the strings. Make knots above and below them to keep them in place at the ends of the strings. The six knots are indicated by numbers on the diagram on the next page.

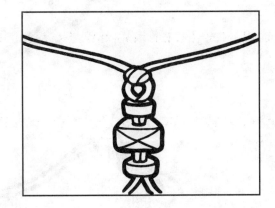

   Time to give them a click-clack!

Worry Bead Pattern

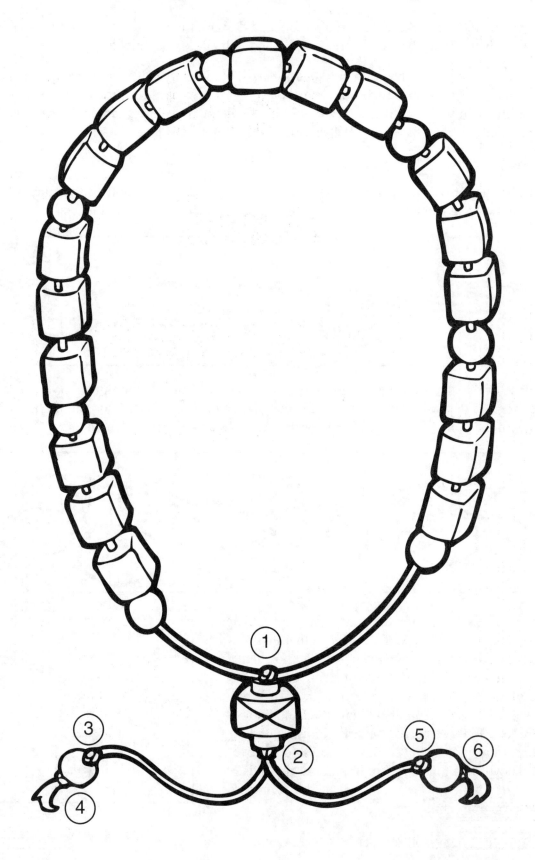

44

Food and Festivals

Greek Holidays

The Greeks enjoy festivals and holidays. There are many traditional holidays in Greece, especially because of the saints' days during the year. Some holidays are followed more in some parts of Greece than in other parts of the country. Because Greece is made up of so many small islands and sections, different traditions became popular in different areas.

The days on the list in bold print are the ones that are recognized as national holidays that would include the closing of businesses and schools.

January 1: St. Basil's Day and Agios Vasileios or Protohronia

January 6: Theofania (Epiphany)

February 2: Ypapanti (Candlemas)

Easter Season

 first Sunday before Lent: Apokries (Carnival Sunday)

 seven Sundays before Easter: Kathari Deftera (Clean Monday)

Holy Week: Megali Evdomada

Palm Sunday: Kyriaki ton Vaion

Maundy Thursday: Megali Pempti

Good Friday: Megali Paraskevi

Easter Sunday: Megali Savvato and Pascha

Easter Sunday: Pascha

March 25: Independence Day and Evangelismos

April 23: Agios Georgios (St. George's Day)

May 1: Portomagia (May Day or Labor Day)

May 21: Agios Konstantinos kai Agia Eleni (St. Constantines's Day)

40 Days after Easter: Analipsi (Ascension)

7 weeks after Orthodox Easter: Pentikosti (Penticost or Whitsunday)

The following Monday: Agiou Pnevmatos (Feast of the Holy Spirit, Whitmonday)

Mid-June to mid-September: Athens Festival

June 24: Klidonas (Chaia, Crete)

June 24: Agios Ioanis (St. John's Day)

June 29: Agioi Apostoloi Petros kai Pavlos (St. Peter's and Paul)

June 30: Agioo Apostoloi (Holy Apostles)

Greek Holidays *(cont.)*

July 14: Agios Nikodimos (St. Nicodemas)

July 17: Agia Marina (St. Marian)

July 18–20: Profitis Ilias (Prophet Elijah)

July 25–28: Agiou Panteleimonos Festival

July and August: Rethymno Festival

August 1–19: Simonideia Festival

August: Ippokrateia Cultural Festival

First week of August: Dionysia Festival

August 6: Metamorfosi (transformation of Christ)

August 15: Koimisis tis Theotokou (assumption of the Virgin Mary)

September 8: Gennisis tis Theotokou (birth of the Virgin Mary)

September 14: Ypsosis tou Timiou Stavrou (Exaltation of the True Cross)

October 26; Agios Dimitrios (St. Dimitri)

October 28: Ochi Day (Greeks said no to surrender to Mussolini)

November 8: Ton Taxiarchon Michail Kai Gavriil (Archangels Michael and Gabriel); Important Name Day.

November 21: Eisodia tis Theotokou (Presentation of the Virgin Mary in the Temple)

December 6: Agios Nikolaos (St. Nickolas)

December 12: Agios Spyridon (St. Spyridon)

December 25: Christougenna (Christmas)

December 26: Synaxis tis Theotokou (meeting of the Virgin's entourage)

Activity

Appoint one member of your class the "Keeper of the Calendar." This student's responsibility will be to make a calendar with the Greek holidays listed on each day. Each morning the Keeper of the Calendar will announce to the class the holiday for that day. Don't forget to announce Name Days, also.

Pascha

Pascha or Easter is the most important religious day of the year in the Greek Orthodox Church. It is to remember Jesus' resurrection on the third day after his crucifixion.

Prior to the Lenten season, a three-week party known as Carnival lets people enjoy the foods they will soon give up. Children are given long balloons to hit people with in jest.

The 40 days before Pascha is a time of fasting known as the "Lenten season." It starts with "Clean Monday" and families will take picnics of simple foods to the country. Many Greeks will give up meat, olive oil, wine, and dairy products until Easter. Some will give up all food on Good Friday.

On Good Friday the churches are decorated with black drapery. Almost everyone takes the day off from work. The mood is very somber. It appears that everyone is in mourning.

Then begins the processions of Holy Saturday. People leave the church in darkness looking for Christ's body. At midnight the priest lights a new candle and announces, "Christo anesti" (Christ is risen). The congregation lights candles from his and thus begins a beautiful procession of people in the glow of candles, with bells ringing and fireworks exploding. They will take the soot from their candle and make the symbol of the cross on their front sidewalk.

They will wake up early to attend church services and wear their finest clothes. Some women will even wear traditional costumes with coin necklaces and brightly colored aprons.

The traditional dinner includes lamb since Jesus was called the "Lamb of God."

The children like the fun of breaking open the Easter eggs which are dyed red. Breaking open the eggs represent the freeing of Christ from his tomb.

Would it be hard to give up something you liked for forty days?

Have you ever tasted lamb?

Christmas in Greece

Christmas is more than just a day in Greece. Christmas is a season that extends from the Feast of St. Nicholas on December 6 until the Feast of the Epiphany on January 6. During that time the people of Greece sing beautiful carols, called *kalandas*, and enjoy a time of feasting and eating Christmas cookies called *melomacarona*. Christmas is a solemn, religious festival in Greece.

Gifts are not exchanged on Christmas Day. That is a day for going to church and spending time with the family. Gifts are usually exchanged on St. Basil's Day, which is January 1. The Greeks observe the 12 days of Christmas, from December 25 to January 6.

During the 12 days of Christmas, you will not see a Christmas tree in a traditional Greek home. The symbol for the season is a bowl of water! Families keep a shallow wooden bowl of water on a table. Across the rim of the bowl is a string or wire. Hanging from the string is a sprig of basil wrapped around a small cross. The basil hangs in the water so that it will stay fresh during the 12 days. During that time, someone in the house will take the sprig of basil out of the bowl, dip it in holy water, and sprinkle the house to keep it safe from little spirits called *kallikantzari*.

Kallikantzari are similar to elves, but they do not make or bring gifts. They bring mischief. There are many folk tales about the *kallikantzari* and the mischief that they can cause in a house. Some say that they cause milk to go sour, or they might cause fires to go out. The *kallikantzari* sneak into people's houses through the chimneys, so during the 12 days of Christmas, it is traditional to keep a Yule log burning in the fireplace, often with a mixture of herbs to keep out the little troublemakers.

St. Nicholas is important in Greece because he is the patron saint of sailors. Greece is dependent upon the sea and sailing for its survival. Many people are sailors, and the boats never leave shore without an icon of St. Nicholas aboard. St. Nicholas does not bring gifts on Christmas, but he protects the people on the sea throughout the year.

Children go from house to house singing *kalandas*. The children will offer their compliments to the house, then the people living there will give the children sweets and biscuits. Today, the children sometimes receive coins.

A traditional food for Christmas is the *christopsomo* or "Christ bread." This bread is baked from very fine ingredients and is decorated with symbols that represent the family and its profession. The traditional meat for a Christmas meal is roast pig, but turkey is becoming more popular in some areas.

Christmas is the second most important holiday in Greece. Easter is more important, but Christmas gives the Greek people the pleasures of food, family, and traditions.

St. Basil's Cake (Vasilopitta)

On New Year's Eve in Greece, children wait anxiously for St. Basil's cake because they know they might find money inside.

Why would there be money inside a cake? Well, that comes from a long and interesting tradition.

One of the most important men in the Greek Orthodox Church history is St. Basil. In Greek his name is Agios Vasileios. He was a very kind man. St. Basil was always concerned for the poor and homeless people of his country. He took care of them. He started hospitals for the poor and was the first person to open orphanages for homeless children.

Many, many years ago, St. Basil was the Archbishop of Caesarea in the province of Cappodocia. The king of that province did not agree with St. Basil and his teachings. The king threatened to invade Caesarea and take all of the belongings and possessions of the people who lived there.

St. Basil did not want the people of his town to suffer. He devised a plan to help the people. He called together all of the wealthy citizens of Caesarea. He asked them to donate great amounts of money and possessions to give to the king. He hoped in this way to prevent an invasion of the area.

St. Basil took all of the treasures to the soldier that the king had sent to invade the town. St. Basil presented the treasures to the soldier, but he also talked to him. He told the soldier that no matter how much the king threatened his people, they would not give up their beliefs. The soldier was so impressed by St. Basil that he did not take the money and other treasures and the people of the town were not bothered by the king anymore.

But St. Basil had a problem. Now he had a great amount of money and jewelry and other possessions that belonged to the wealthy people, and he did not know how to tell what belonged to which person. He came up with a plan. He baked cakes and put jewelry and money into each cake. He handed the cakes out to the people. Then a miracle happened. When the people cut into the cakes, each person found his or her own possessions in the cake!

Today, it is a tradition to bake a cake on St. Basil's day and hide a coin inside. The person who finds the coin will have good luck during the new year.

There is a very particular way in which the cake is handed out to family members. First of all the cake is cut into pieces. The first piece is cut for Jesus, God, or St. Basil. Pieces of the cake are distributed to the family members according to their ages. The oldest first, then down to the youngest. Some families cut pieces for the pets of the family. The last and the largest piece is given to the poor because St. Basil always thought of the poor and hungry.

Now you can enjoy the tradition of St. Basil's cake:

Directions

1. Purchase a white cake box mix. Prepare according to the directions on the box but use orange juice in place of water.

2. Place a clean coin (wrapped inside a piece of aluminum foil) inside the batter and bake the cake according to the box instructions.

3. Sprinkle the top of the cake with confectioner's sugar or frost it with a thin white icing.

4. Decorate with the numbers of the year.

5. Almonds and sesame seeds can also be sprinkled on top. Some people even garnish the top of the cake with an olive branch.

6. Eat carefully!

Name Days and Names

Each Saint is assigned a day of the year in the Greek Orthodox Church. The members of the church celebrate their special saint's day, after whom they are named. On the designated day, friends visit to congratulate the person who is honored. There is always food and dancing. People will go to visit several homes if their patron saint is that same day.

Not only people have name days but also towns. Each Greek town has a patron saint and a celebration. Processions in which images of the saint are carried take place through the town. Prayer meetings are held to honor him or her. The entire town will enjoy the festivities with good food and music. It is a festive and thankful time for Greek families.

Do you think you would like this custom? Why or why not?

Is this a good way to remember important religious people by celebrating on their Saint's Day?

Would you like or dislike having a saint's name given to you?

What makes a person a saint?

Names are very important to Greek families. The firstborn son will probably be given his father's name or, in other words, his grandfather's name. The first daughter then would be given her paternal grandmother's name. If the grandfather has many children named after him, the family might give the honor to the mother's father and mother.

What would your name be if you were named for your grandparent?

Many Greek names describe some characteristics about the person. They started out as nicknames, which their grandsons inherited and took the place of their family name.

Do you have a nickname? Would it make a good family name?

What if you shared your birthday with everyone else who had the same name? In Greece, people usually don't celebrate their birthdays after they reach the age of 12. Instead, they celebrate a Name Day.

Almost every day in the Greek year is dedicated to a saint. Most of the people in Greece are named for saints or important people in Greek history or mythology. So your Name Day would fall on the day of the saint or famous person for whom you were named.

Here is an example.

January 20 is the day for St. John the Baptist. If your name is John, then you would celebrate your Name Day on January 20. The day you were born would not be as important. Everyone else named for St. John would celebrate on that day, too. So you would go to the homes of other people named John, or they would come to your house, and you would have small gifts and cakes. Gifts are not as important as they are on your birthdays in the U.S. People are more interested in just remembering each other and wishing each other well.

On your Name Day, you would tell other people, "Giortazo simera." This means "I am celebrating today." The other person would reply, "Chronia polla." This means, "Many years." It is like saying, "Many happy returns."

On the next page is a list of some of the Name Days in Greece. Find the name day for each member of your class. Write the names on a calendar and remember to greet your classmates with the traditional Greek greeting on their Name Days. (**Note:** There is a possibility that some names may not appear on the list. Ask students to select a name of a friend or relative instead.)

Name Days List

Here is a list of Name Days. See if you can find your name and the names of your friends. Write the names on a calendar in the classroom.

January

Date	Names
1	Boniface
4	Evan, Eveline
6	Eugenia, Gladys
9	Stephen
11	Georgiana
14	Basil, William
15	Sylvester
20	John
21	Esther, Hester
27	Adam, Isaac, Nina

February

Date	Names
1	Marcarius
3	Anna
4	Timothy
6	Xenia
7	Gregory, Margaret, Marjorie
8	May
10	Ephraim
13	Theresa
14	Felicity
16	Simeon
19	Dorothy, Dora, Dorcas, Beulah
23	Paula, Pauline
24	Blaise

March

Date	Names
3	Leo, Leon, Lionel, Leonie
7	Maurice
17	Juliana
30	Alexis

April

Date	Names
1	Darcie, Vivian
5	Lydia
8	Ignatius, Larissa
14	Maria, Mary, Molly, Marilyn
15	Veronica
17	Joe
27	Martin
28	Prudence
29	Charissa

May

Date	Names
5	Nathan, Theodore
6	Alexandria, Georgia, George, Sandra
7	Betsy, Betty, Elsie, Isabel
8	Mark, Marcia
11	Jason
13	Dina, James, Rachel
14	Jeremy, Tamara
21	Constantine
22	Christopher, Christian
23	Simon, Isadora
25	Germain
30	June
31	Claudette, Claudia

June

Date	Names
3	Helen, Helena, Nelly
14	Justine, Kay, Lucius, Carita
17	Manuel
19	Valeria
20	Priscilla
22	Martha, Miriam
24	Elizabeth, Zacharias, Barnabas, Barnaby, Bartholomew, Nathaniel
26	Antonia
28	Jerome
30	Emanuel, Manuel

Name Day List *(cont.)*

July

Date	Names
2	Jude, Judith
4	Julian, Julius
7	Jane, Janet, Jeanne, Jenny, Joan
9	Dennis
11	David
12	Peter, Paul
14	Damian
18	Inez
24	Aileen, Elaine, Ellen
25	Hilary
29	Julia, Ruth

August

Date	Names
4	Madeline, Maude
6	Christine
7	Annette, Olive
14	Achim
21	Amelai, Emily
22	Mathias
23	Lawrence
24	Susana, Susan
30	Myron, Myrtel
31	Laura

September

Date	Names
2	Samuel
3	Thaddeus
8	Adrian, Adrienne, Natalie
10	Nancy
12	Alexander
14	Joshua
16	Phoebe
17	Hermione
18	Zachary, Elizabeth
19	Michael
22	Joachim, Joad, Anna, Hannah
28	Barry, Deborah
30	Charity, Edna, Faith, Hope, Nadine, Sonia, Sophia, Vera

October

Date	Names
19	Thomas
20	Serge
22	Abraham, Rebecca, Sally, Sarah
26	Benjamin
28	Lucian
31	Luke

November

Date	Names
1	Joel
4	Anastasia
5	Jacob
10	Terrence, Eunice, Naomi
11	Marian
16	Joseph, Josephine
18	Jonas, Linus
21	Mitchell
23	Victoria
24	Victor, Vincent, Stephanie
27	Phillip
29	Matthew

December

Date	Names
1	Roman, Zacheus
7	Katherine, Catherine
13	Andrew
17	Barbara
19	Nicholas
22	Anita
23	Angelina
25	Spiridon
26	Orestes, Lucia
27	Stefanos
30	Daniel

Greek Wedding Traditions

In Greece an engaged couple exchanges rings at their engagement party in front of all their family. There is always a big dinner, and this ceremony is as binding as the wedding itself.

On the Wednesday before the wedding, the custom of "starting the leaven" is begun. The couple will sieve the flour for the bread while the family looks on and throws coins into the sieve for good luck.

On Friday the tradition called "filling the sacks" occurs. The bride's mother puts a copper pan in a sack and the bride fills it and other sacks with her possessions while friends and relatives throw coins. The groom and the bride's father are busy sending pitchers of wine to their friends and relatives around the village with an invitation to come to the wedding.

On Saturday, the bride will invite her friends to the wedding by sending sweets.

The "koumbaros" is the sponsor for the wedding and is usually the godfather of the groom or another man who may be given the honor. Some say he is more important than the priest or the groom.

On Sunday in a small town, the wedding procession starts at the groom's house where a wedding flag is raised. The flag bearer will lead the priest, groom, and his family over to the bride's house. The bride's mother will offer the groom a drink and special herbs to wear on the lapel of his suit. The bride is escorted by her father to the church and the rest of the family follows.

In Ancient Greece, wedding ceremonies were always after dark. The veiled bride came to the groom's home in a chariot. Her family brought gifts. During the ceremony, the bride would eat a piece of fruit to symbolize that she would be taken care of by her husband. Torches were lit and music was played to send evil spirits away. Prized gifts were mirrors, baskets, jewelry, perfume, and furniture.

In other parts of Greece, the ceremony was simple. The bride and groom would struggle. He would then show his strength and toss her over his shoulder to carry her off to his home.

In the Greek Orthodox Church today, there are many traditions. Following is a brief description of some of them. The marriage ceremony involves many religious symbols.

- The wedding couple exchanges rings three times. This symbolizes the union of the couple and that they are made more complete and stronger by their marriage.
- The wedding couple lights and holds candles throughout the service.
- They join their right hands to show togetherness.
- The crowning of the bride and groom is one of the most unique traditions. During the wedding ceremony, the bride and groom wear crowns that are linked together by a ribbon. The connecting ribbon symbolizes their new union as husband and wife. The crowns represent their new position as the king and queen of their own home.
- They drink from the same cup.
- They take a ceremonial walk. It represents their first steps together as a married couple.
- The new bride and groom receive a blessing from the priest.

Ochi Day – A National Holiday for Saying "NO!"

On October 28, the people of Greece celebrate that one man said, "No." It is one of Greece's most important national holidays. Schools and businesses are closed. There are parades and festivals. People take the entire day off, just because one man said, "No!" in 1940. Who was this man, and why did he say, "No!"? Why do the people of Greece commemorate this day?

In 1940 the world was involved in World War II. Hitler was the leader of Germany, and he was trying to control all of Europe. He was taking over one country at a time as he moved across the continent.

Italy was an ally of Germany. The leader of Italy was a man named Benito Mussolini. The Italians tried to occupy Greece, and the prime minister of Greece said, "No!" This man's name was Ioannis Metaxas. His answer to Mussolini represented the pride and independence of the Greek people.

The Greeks not only said "no" to Hitler and Mussolini, but the Greek army drove the Italians back through most of Albania. Because Greece would not let the Italians and the Germans move through their country, it is possible that World War II ended sooner than it might have otherwise. All of this was because one man and one small country were not afraid to say "no" to a more powerful country.

Ochi is pronounced "o-HEE."

Find out what these words mean: *commemorate, ally, continent, Europe.*

Look up some information about these men: Ioannis Metaxis, Benito Mussolini, Adolf Hitler.

When is it good to say, "No!"? Write a story about saying "no" and how it might help someone.

Think about these holidays in the United States:

- Veteran's Day
- Independence Day
- Martin Luther King Jr. Day
- Flag Day
- Presidents' Day

How do these days represent brave people? Who were these brave people? What did they do that was brave?

A Greek Cookout – Shish Kebob

Souvlaki is marinated meat on skewers which is cooked over an open fire or barbequed. This is often called "shish kebob."

Ingredients and Materials

- wooden skewer sticks (one for a child, 2 or 3 per adult)

The amounts below are approximate for each skewer:

- cherry tomatoes—1 or 2 per person

- onions and tomatoes—6 (quartered)

- mushrooms—1 or 2 large, fresh per person

- marinated meat—lamb, chicken or beef—cubed into 2-inch (5-cm) pieces, 3 to 4 pieces per person

- whole bay leaves—3 whole per person

- peppers—5 or 6, into 2-inch (5-cm) pieces

- canned potatoes—1 can for every 4 or 5 people (optional)

Directions

1. Encourage your class to at least each of all the vegetables. Alternate one vegetable between each piece of meat. *Hint:* Soak the wooden sticks for 15 minutes before cooking. This will keep the sticks from burning. This will make about 10 to 15 skewers.

2. Marinate the meat for 4 to 5 hours in the refrigerator in this mixture:
   - ½ cup (120 mL) melted butter and ½ cup (120 mL) olive oil
   - 1 cup (240 mL) lemon juice
   - 2 tbs. (30 mL) oregano
   - ½ tsp. (2.5 mL) pepper

3. Cook the skewers over hot coals or broil. Baste continuously with the extra marinade and turn skewers frequently to cook everything evenly. (*Optional:* Enjoy your shish kebob over a bed of rice pilaf.)

56

Stuffed Grape Leaves

This is a traditional Greek dish that can be served either hot or cold. Stuffed grape leaves are like little packages of rice and meat filling. Served hot, they make a great meal. Served cold, they make a picnic meal. Other names for this treat are *yaprakia* or *dolmas*.

Ingredients

- 1½ lbs. (680 grams) ground beef
- 2 cups rice (raw, long-grained)
- 1 finely chopped medium onion
- ¾ cup (177 mL) olive oil
- 3 tbs. (44 mL) crushed, dried mint
- 1 tsp. (5 mL) salt
- 1 tsp. (5 mL) pepper
- 1 can tomato juice (6 oz. or 177 mL)
- 1 jar grapevine leaves in brine (2 lbs. or 907 g)
- 3 fresh lemons (for juice)
- 2 eggs
- 1 three-quart pot

Directions

1. Combine the first eight ingredients in a large bowl. Mix thoroughly, using your hands.

2. Unroll two rolls of grape leaves from the jar. Rinse and drain. Line the bottom of a pot with three or four leaves. Use a teaspoon of filling for each leaf. Fill the leaves according to the diagram on the next page.

3. Fill the pot with the rolled leaves, placing them tightly together in concentric circles. When the pot is full, barely cover the leaves with cold water. Squeeze the juice of one lemon on top. Put a sandwich plate or saucer on top of the leaves to hold the bundles in place so they won't unroll.

4. Cover the pot and bring it to a slow boil. Simmer about 1½ hours or until the rice is tender. Add more water if you need to. Remove from the heat and let set for 15 minutes before serving.

5. Make an avgolemono sauce to go over the stuffed leaves. Separate the two eggs. Whip the whites until stiff. Add the yolks and beat until blended. Add the lemon juice of two lemons and beat until just mixed. Serve the stuffed leaves with the avgolemono sauce. (**Note:** The avgolemon sauce is optional.) The stuffed leaves can also be served with yogurt.

6. These make good finger food for the market or the Olympics. Students will have fun learning to fold the grape leaves around the filling.

Stuffed Grape Leaves *(cont.)*

Teacher's Note

This activity is good practice for following written instructions from reading a diagram. This activity requires students to develop good eye-hand coordination. If you do not actually want to make the recipe, you can have the students cut out grape leaves and learn to fold them anyway. They could make little packages of candy or other surprises.

Follow these steps to make your stuffed grape leaves:

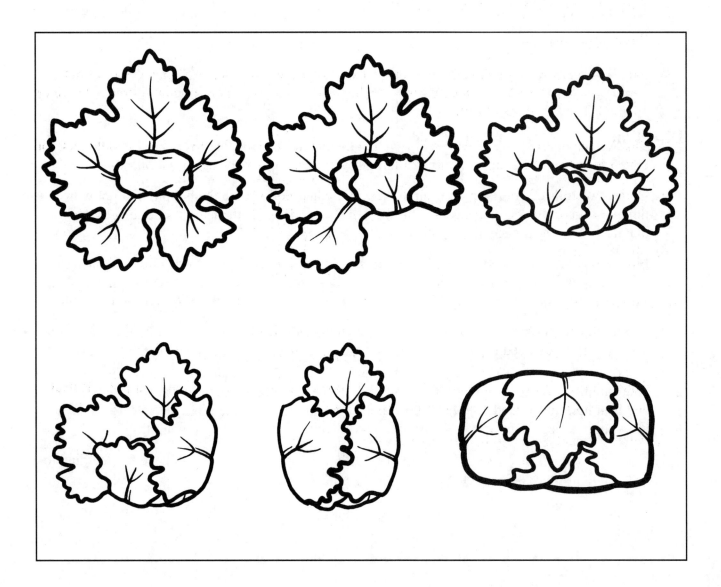

58

Olga's Baklava

Ingredients

- 2 lbs. (907 grams) filo dough
- 1 lb. (453.5 grams) and 1 stick of unsalted butter
- 2 cups (473 mL) of chopped walnuts
- 2 tsp. (9.85 mL) cinnamon
- 1 pinch of cloves

Directions

1. Butter bottom of 13" x 9" (33 cm x 23 cm) pan.

2. Butter each sheet.

3. Put 10 sheets of filo dough on bottom of the pan. After the tenth sheet sprinkle a layer of nuts, cinnamon, and cloves. Continue layering in this manner until you have used all of the nuts. Save 10 good sheets of dough for the top.

4. Bake on the bottom rack of the oven for about 20 minutes at 350° F. Move to the middle rack for 1 hour at 350° F. Cut pieces almost all the way through.

5. See the pattern for cutting the dough into the traditional diamond shape.

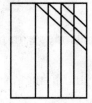

6. Mix the syrup.

Ingredients for Syrup

- 5 cups (1.2 L) of sugar
- 2½ cups (591 mL) of water
- juice of 1 lemon
- 1 cup (236.5 mL) honey

Combine the ingredients and bring to a boil. Boil for five minutes to thicken. Turn off the heat and let the mixture cool. Pour over the hot baklava.

7. Allow to stand overnight before serving.

Marty Sulek's Plaka Tsatziki (Cucumber Yogurt Dip)

Tsatziki is used in many Greek recipes as a tasty addition to lamb or other meats. It is the sauce that is used in gyro sandwiches and as a dip.

Ingredients

- 1 quart (946 mL) of plain yogurt
- 1 seedless cucumber
- 4–5 cloves of chopped garlic
- 1 scallion, thinly sliced
- ½ cup (118 mL) of virgin olive oil
- ¼ cup (59 mL) of fresh dill (if possible)
- ¼ tsp. (1.2 mL) of salt
- ½ tsp. (2.5 mL) fresh ground pepper
- serve with pita chips

Directions

1. Place two layers of cheesecloth in a strainer.
2. Add the yogurt and make a sack by tying the cheesecloth at the top.
3. Let it drain for about three hours at room temperature.
4. Peel and dice the cucumber.
5. Add half the cucumber to the blender with the garlic and lightly blend. It should still be a bit chunky.
6. Put the mixture in a bowl and fold in the rest of the ingredients and add remaining diced cucumber.
7. Chill for an hour before serving.

This makes about two cups. You may need to double the recipe for a large class.

You can make chips by buying pita bread and slicing it into eight wedges. Heat the wedges for 10 minutes at 350°F for crispy chips. You can microwave them instead if you prefer soft chips.

Eat Greek and Eat Healthy

Greek salad is a favorite in many restaurants. The fresh ingredients of this salad reflect the agriculture of the Greek islands. Olives are common in many Greek dishes. Cucumbers and peppers are easy to grow in the Greek climate. Wine vinegar, olive oil, and oregano are flavors that are found frequently in the islands. The anchovies come from the sea, and feta cheese is a Greek specialty.

Salads from any land reflect the products that are available. Enjoy this healthy way to taste a little bit of Greece.

Greek Tossed Salad

Ingredients

- 1 head of lettuce
- 1 peeled and sliced cucumber
- 1 green pepper, chopped
- 4 scallions, chopped
- 12 or more Calamata olives
- wine vinegar and olive oil (equal parts)
- 12 Salonika peppers (optional)
- 6 anchovies (optional)
- feta cheese
- 1 tsp. (5 mL) oregano
- salt and pepper to taste
- crusty bread

Directions

Tear lettuce into small pieces. Add cucumber, peppers, scallions, olives, anchovies, and oregano. Sprinkle with spices. Drizzle olive oil and vinegar to taste. Add salt and pepper to taste. Toss and serve with Olga's Koulourakia. See recipe on the next page.

Eat Greek and Eat Healthy *(cont.)*

Olga's Koulourakia

Ingredients

- ½ lb. (227 grams) butter
- ½ lb. (227 grams) shortening
- 2 tsp. (10 mL) baking powder
- ½ tsp. (2.5 mL) baking soda
- sugar

- 8 eggs, separated
- orange rind of 2 oranges
- 9½ to 10 cups (2.25 mL to 2.4 mL) of flour
- sesame seeds
- milk

Directions

Beat butter in mixer, add sugar, and mix well. Mix baking powder and baking soda and whisk together. Add butter mixture. Beat egg whites until fluffy and slowly fold into mixture. Then add orange rind and flour. Dough should be of smooth consistency and easy to roll (and not be holely). Do not use too much flour. Place shaped dough on ungreased baking pan. Mix egg yolk, a little sugar, and a bit of milk (best to mix with fork) and spread over Koulouria tops. Sprinkle with sesame seeds. Bake at 350°F for about 15–20 minutes or until golden brown.

62

Greek Lemon Soup (Avgolemono)

This tasty dish is the best known of all Greek soups.

This is a great class project for a cold day. Have two large crock pots ready for the day. Divide the ingredients among your volunteers.

Ingredients

- 2 lemons
- a 42 oz. (1.24 L) can of chicken broth
- 1 cup orzo macaroni
  (or ½ cup (118 mL) uncooked long grain rice)
- 4 eggs

- 1 cup cream
- ½ tsp. (2.5 mL) salt
- pepper for taste
- 3 tbs. (44 mL) butter

Directions

1. Juice the lemons and set aside.
2. Put broth in crock pots and bring to a boil.
3. Stir in orzo or rice, salt, and pepper. Cook for about 20 minutes or until the rice or macaroni is tender.
4. Turn heat down to low.
5. Separate the eggs.
6. Beat the whites until peaks are formed.
7. Add lemon juice.
8. Slowly add a ½ cup (118 mL) of soup, cream, and beaten egg yolks to the egg-lemon mixture.
9. Add to crock pot for 5 minutes, add butter (if desired).
10. Serve immediately so that the soup is still frothy.
11. Serve with crusty bread.

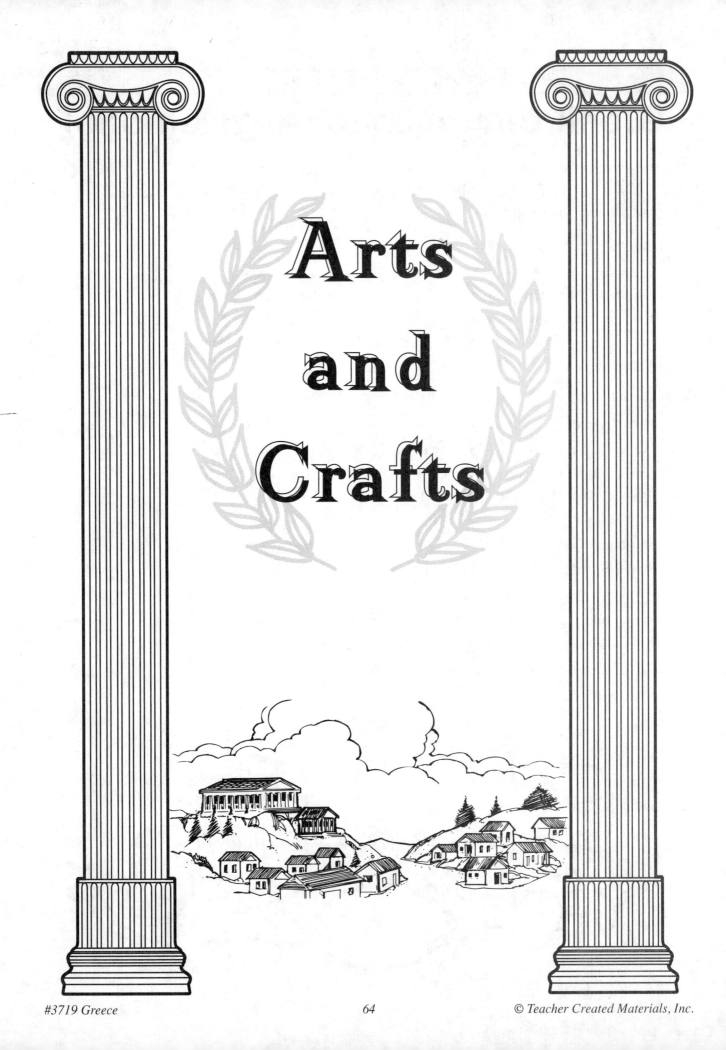

Arts and Crafts

Count Your Way Through Greece

Count Your Way Through Greece is a charming book that works as a good introduction to Greece. This book was written by Jim Haskins and Kathleen Benson and was illustrated by Janice Lee Porter. It was published by Carolrhoda Book, Inc., in Minneapolis, 1996.

This book teaches students to count from one to ten in Greek. It also has very nice pictures of people and items from Greece. Each letter is associated with some aspect of Greek life and covers everything from religion to mythology and crafts.

Use the book as a beginning activity. Have the children discuss the variety of things mentioned in the book. Explain to them that Greece is a very old country with many ancient traditions and beliefs.

Before reading the book, ask students what they already know about Greece. After reading the book to them, have them tell you what they learned. Which things about Greece surprised them?

The book is a good starting point for other activities. You can use ideas and topics to spark interest in report topics.

Tie the book into the My Count to Ten in Greek activity on page 66 in which students complete a count to 10 book and illustrate it.

When the class is finished with the Greece unit, students can make their own count-to-ten books about what they learn from their study of Greece. You may also want them to write a count-to-ten book about their own country or community.

As you read the book, have the students listen for these things:

- How is religion treated differently in Greece than in the United States?
- Why is the sea important to the people of Greece?
- How many sides do you think a pentagon has?

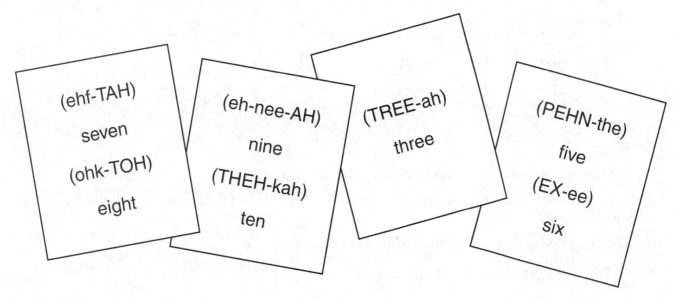

(ehf-TAH)
seven
(ohk-TOH)
eight

(eh-nee-AH)
nine
(THEH-kah)
ten

(TREE-ah)
three

(PEHN-the)
five
(EX-ee)
six

Greek Word Book

Directions

1. Duplicate page 67.

2. Fold the page in half lengthwise and crease.

3. Fold in half widthwise, then fold again. Unfold completely. The paper will have eight sections.

4. Refold along center fold widthwise. Have fold at top of paper. Cut along the vertical fold to the next horizontal fold halfway down. Unfold.

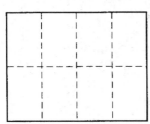 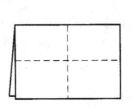 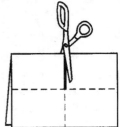

5. Refold lengthwise. Push ends together so that the center bows out on either side. Fold pages so that they all go in the same directions to make the pages of the book.

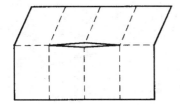 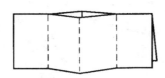 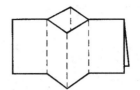

Activities

1. Students can color the book and add pictures to the pages.

2. You may want to have the students make their books out of plain paper and write the words on the pages along with their own pictures.

3. Have the students practice counting with each other.

4. Have the students look up Greek words in a dictionary and make another book using their own words.

My Count to Ten in Greek Book

ten (THEH-kah) nine (eh-nee-AH)	eight (ohk-TOH) seven (ehf-TAH)
My name is _____	six (EX-ee) five (PEHN-the)
one (EH-nah)	four (THE-she-rah)
two (THEE-oh)	three (TREE-ah)

Greek Pottery

The art of pottery began on the southern mainland and the Greek islands over seven thousand years ago. Clay became beautiful vases, vessels for storing food and water, lamps, and children's toys. Pottery was so popular that it was exported all around the Mediterranean and Black Seas.

The toys were often dolls or puppets. They have been found in the graves of children since it was believed that the children would have them in the next world. When children turned about 12 years old, they were considered to be grown up. They were expected to take their toys to their temple during a special religious ceremony and offer them to the god Apollo and his sister, Artemis.

A clay jar (like the one shown on page 69) is called an "amphora." The plural of amphora is "amphorae." They were used for many purposes in ancient times. Since their shape is exactly alike on both sides, they are symmetrical.

During the 7,000 years of making pottery, people tried new things. One style of pottery was all black designs or figures. Red clay paint was used and silhouettes were made by carving into the clay. Another style is called "geometric." Rulers or compasses were used to make orderly patterns.

Look at some reference resources for examples of designs that the Greek potters used on their pottery. You will see that they show pictures of people doing everyday activities. That is why we know so much about life in Ancient Greece today.

The painters would paint figures, flowers, sea life, animals like lions, panthers, or birds. Some would even depict monsters and other beasts from well-known stories. Think of a movie you have enjoyed that has animals . . . did you ever see these animals on a cup or plate?

Designing Greek Pottery

Try this technique to make a symmetrical drawing of an amphora. Fold a piece of paper in half. Draw the shape shown on the next page. Cut it out. Trace around this stencil on a folded piece of black or terracotta paper. Open up the paper to see the complete shape of the amphora.

Using white pencil or chalk, add a design that tells something about your everyday life.

That is what the Greek potters often did and why we know so much about them today. They painted sports scenes, weddings, and funerals. If it were not for the pottery, people wouldn't know as much about their everyday life, since paintings didn't survive. Some of the pottery was found in tombs. And, even the broken pieces, called "pot shards" have been put back together to solve the mystery of what the Greek people did thousands of years ago.

Use the designs on the next three pages to make other pottery. You can also use the designs to explore Greek archeology.

Greek Pottery Patterns

Use this pattern to make your own amphora. Trace this design on a piece of folded black or terra cotta construction paper. Add your own design about everyday life.

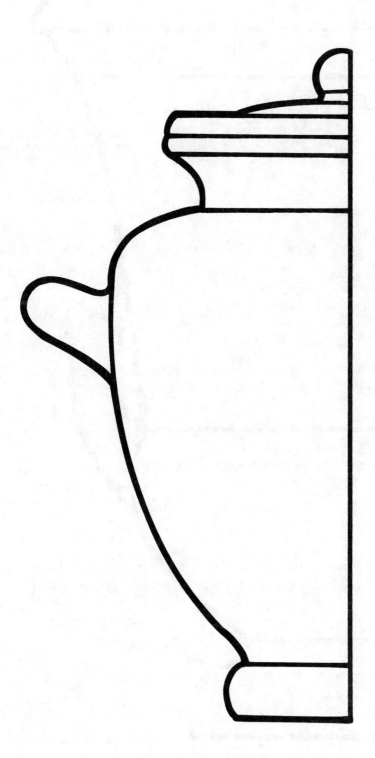

Greek Pottery Patterns *(cont.)*

Greek Pottery Patterns *(cont.)*

Pottery Jumble –
An Archeological Challenge

Much of what we know about Ancient Greece has been learned through the study of archeology. Archeologists examine pottery, jewelry, buildings, and other artifacts from past civilizations. They can tell what life was like for the people who lived thousands of years ago. Scientists can tell what people ate and how they cooked their food. They can tell from pictures how people dressed and wore their hair. They know what kinds of musical instruments they played and what kinds of toys the children had. Archeology is an exciting and interesting science.

When archeologists look for remains of old civilizations and other artifacts from the past, they go to a "dig." A dig is a place where the conditions are right for remains. In Greece there are many digs.

Archeologists do not just go somewhere and start digging. They have a plan and a particular way of looking for things. They decide where a good place to search is. Then they mark off that area in a grid. A grid divides an area into small squares. Each square of the grid has a letter and a number. When archeologists find something in a particular square, they can accurately record where they were and what they found there. Then when the excavation is finished, all of the pieces from the squares can be put together like a giant jigsaw puzzle.

You can take your class on a mini-archeological dig. Here is what you will need:

Materials

- large, shallow plastic bin or cardboard box (like an under-the-bed storage box)
- enough sand to fill the box
- pottery pieces (laminate and cut up the pottery pictures on the preceding pages)
- string
- tape
- some old paint brushes of various sizes (be sure to include some very small ones)
- a piece of paper
- a pencil or pen
- a bucket or another box

Directions

1. Fill the box with sand. Put the pottery pieces into the sand. Be sure to mix up the pieces and scatter them around.
2. Use the string to make a grid across the top of the box. Tape two pieces going lengthwise and three going across. Make sure you space the string evenly so the box is divided into twelve small squares.
3. Have the students draw matching grids on their papers. Label the horizontal rows with letters and the vertical columns with numbers. Your squares will be A1, A2, A3, A4, B1, etc.
4. Instruct the students to carefully brush away the sand in one square until they find something. Tell them to record this on their paper what they found and where they found it. Pour the sand that they take away into a bucket or other container.
5. After the students find all of the pottery pieces, have them reassemble the pottery and display it in the room.

72

Extension Activities for the Pottery Jumble

Encourage the children to take their time and work carefully. Discuss how the age of a find can be determined by how deeply it is buried. Try burying one of the pottery pieces deeper than the others to reinforce this idea.

Try burying one of the pottery pieces relatively intact so that the students can see how a grid will help them get the whole picture when they are done.

Discuss why some pottery pieces remains would be found intact, while others might be found jumbled up or incomplete. Bury one of the pots with some pieces missing. What problems would that cause for archeologists? How would they go about figuring out what the missing pieces were like?

Talk to the students about what they would find on an actual dig. They will be finding pieces of pottery, but on a dig they would find other household items as well.

Try burying other things in the sand. Put in things like plastic bottle caps, paper clips, or Legos®. Talk to the children about why these things would not be buried as deeply as the pottery pieces.

Discuss how the things we use today might become treasures to archeologists of the future.

Have your class make a time capsule. Put in things that are important to them. Have them write about what people will think of their items in 25, 50, or 100 years

Creating a Grecian Work of Art

Greeks have enjoyed using contrasting black and white, or terra cotta and black designs on their pottery for over 2,000 years. Their creations were shipped all over the Mediterranean.

Students can easily re-create the look of this pottery by using a simple technique.

First, ask the students what we can tell about Greek life from looking at the pottery.

If they wanted to tell people of the future about what children were like in the twenty-first century, what would they draw?

You can either have them draw a likeness of an ancient piece or have them create their own design by a picture of an everyday activity.

Have the class look at pottery from these Websites or books to inspire them:

www.hellenic-art.com
www.uky.edu/AS/Classica/shapes.html
www.yasou.org/ancient/pottery.htm

Purchase black etching boards. They come with a wooden stylus. Look in any art catalogue under "Scratch-Art." You can get 12 sheets of 8 ½" x 11" (21.5 cm x 28 cm) for about $4.50.

Sketch the design on a thin type of paper. Attach the design to the black sheet with paper clips. Trace the lines again by pressing the pencil into the paper. You will leave an impression of the drawing.

Next you can use the stylus to remove the black. You can also just let the students use the stylus directly on the black sheet without a preliminary drawing. Older students seem to like to plan a bit.

Another option is to cover a heavy paper (oaktag) or poster board with a terra cotta red crayon. Next coat the crayon with a layer or two of Indian ink. This will stain clothing permanently, so an adult will need to supervise.

After the ink is dry, you can scratch off your design or drawing. You can use the tip of a metal compass or a pointed wooden toothpick. Tell the children not to press too hard or they will also take off the crayon.

Have students display their work around the room or at the class Olympics.

Greek Icons

Icons are paintings of important religious figures used to teach a scripture from the Bible. They were originally made long ago when many people could not read, so they were used to convey a message.

The word *icon* comes from the Greek word *eikon* which means "image." Icons were first made some 500 years after the death of Jesus during the Byzantine Empire and spread to Russia 500 years after that. Iconographers, the name given to these painters, were thought to be "chosen" people and were very respected. The books of valuable tracings were passed from one generation to the next.

Those who paint icons have special rules or "canons" that they follow.

1. Icons are painted on wood boards. A cotton cloth is glued to the board like a canvas and dried. The figure to be painted may be lightly outlined on the board.

2. The first thing to be painted is the halo. It is done with red clay. Thin sheets of 23-karat gold leaf are added to represent the figure's divine light.

3. The background is then painted, and layers of paint are added to the face or figure. The last thing that the artist does is paint the hair and highlight the face, hands, and feet. Many artists use egg tempera that they mix themselves using real egg yolks and pigment.

   They would mix the egg, pigment, and "kvas." Kvas was made from fermented bread and currants. When you look at the older paintings you can appreciate that they didn't just get their paint from a tube. One of the rarest colors in the old icons was the blue that came from a stone called "lapis lazuli." It came all the way from the West Hindu Mountains.

4. A final layer of oil or varnish is applied to protect the painting. It is then left to dry slowly.

5. The icon is often not signed by the artist.

6. The icon will be taken to the church to be blessed by the priest.

Before they begin painting, some iconographers will pray, fast, and have their materials blessed. They may play music that helps them feel spiritually ready.

Greek Icons *(cont.)*

Here is a list of colors commonly used by the iconographers. See if you can match them with what they meant to the artists.

_____ 1. red	a. purity
_____ 2. blue	b. energy
_____ 3. green	c. blood
_____ 4. white	d. heaven
_____ 5. black	e. death
_____ 6. gold	f. life

When you paint which colors make you feel happy? Sad? Excited? Calm or peaceful?

Color the following picture twice using completely different colors to see if the mood or feeling of the picture is changes.

Why do you think that there may have been strict rules about the recopying of the icon paintings? Can colors change the meaning or feeling of the painting? How did your picture change?

- -

Hint: Fold this section under before reproducing.

Answers: 1. c **2.** d **3.** f **4.** a **5.** e **6.** b

         76

Greek Treasure Boxes

On the next page is a pattern for making small boxes. These boxes are fun and easy to make. Students enjoy making them to give to their families and friends.

Materials

- lightweight cardboard
- crayons or markers
- scissors
- glue or tape

Directions

1. Copy the pattern on lightweight cardboard (65#).

2. Have students color the top of the box.

3. Follow the folding instructions:

   - Cutting on the short ends of the paper, make 2½" (6.3 cm) cuts at a distance of 2½" (6.3 cm) from each side of the paper.

   - Fold the long edges of the paper along the lines formed by the cuts.

   - Fold the short edges of the paper up at the ends of the cuts. This will form flaps to use to make the boxes.

4. Tape or glue the flaps on the inside of the box.

5. Make bottoms for the box out of plain sheets of lightweight cardboard.

6. Make the bottoms slightly smaller by cutting ¼" (.6 cm) further on the lines and by trimming off or folding over the excess after folding up the sides.

This pattern is also fun to use with old greeting cards. Use the front of the card to make the top and the inside of the card to make the bottom. You will be surprised at the cute designs and patterns that show up. The greeting inside the card makes a cute note on the inside bottom of the box.

Greek Treasure Boxes *(cont.)*

A Fresh Look at Fresco

The Greeks loved beautiful things and surrounded themselves with art. One popular way of decorating a room or building was to paint the walls. When the Minoan Palace at Knossos on the island of Crete was discovered, ancient wall paintings were uncovered that showed the beauty of the fresco artwork.

Have students look at pictures from the Minoan Palace and other Greek structures. They will find pictures of bulls, dolphins, religious ceremonies, monkeys, exotic plants, octopi, warships, and many other topics. Ask the students what they can learn about the Greeks from looking at these pictures.

Your students can create "mini frescos" to keep and display.

Have each student select a subject for his or her fresco. Keep the subject to one that will be simple to draw and paint.

Materials

- newspaper to cover the working area
- plain paper
- scissors
- pencils
- masking tape
- tempera paints
- quality paint brushes
- mat knife
- Plaster of Paris®
- mixing containers
- spatula
- tongue depressors
- a small cereal box for each project
- small rope or heavy cord for hanging the finished projects

Directions

1. Cut one large side off the cereal box with a mat knife. Tape the remaining corners with masking tape to prevent leaking. Lay the box on its side so that it forms a "tray."

2. Mix the plaster of Paris according to directions in another container. Pour the plaster into the cereal box to a depth of about 1" (2.54 cm).

3. Smooth the top surface of the plaster with a tongue depressor. Make a loop from a 7"–8" (18 cm–20 cm) length of cord, and put the ends into the wet plaster. This will make the hanging loop when the project is dry. Set the plaster aside until it is set.

4. While waiting for the plaster to set up, make the pattern for the design. Cut a piece of plain paper the same size as the plaster. Use a pencil to create the design. When the design is correct, trace very heavily over the outline with a graphite pencil. Soft leads are good too.

5. When the plaster is firmly set, turn it out of the box. Turn the pattern over onto the front of the plaster. Transfer the design by drawing over the outline on the wrong side. If the outline isn't clear, go over the lines with a pencil.

6. Use the tempera paints to finish the design in pretty colors.

7. Use the loop on the back to hang the finished fresco for all to enjoy.

The word *fresco* means "fresh." This was because frescos are usually painted on fresh, or not quite dry, plaster with paints dissolved in water. The technique allows the paint to become part of the dried wall. Depending upon the timing of your project, you can have the students paint on plaster in varying stages of dryness.

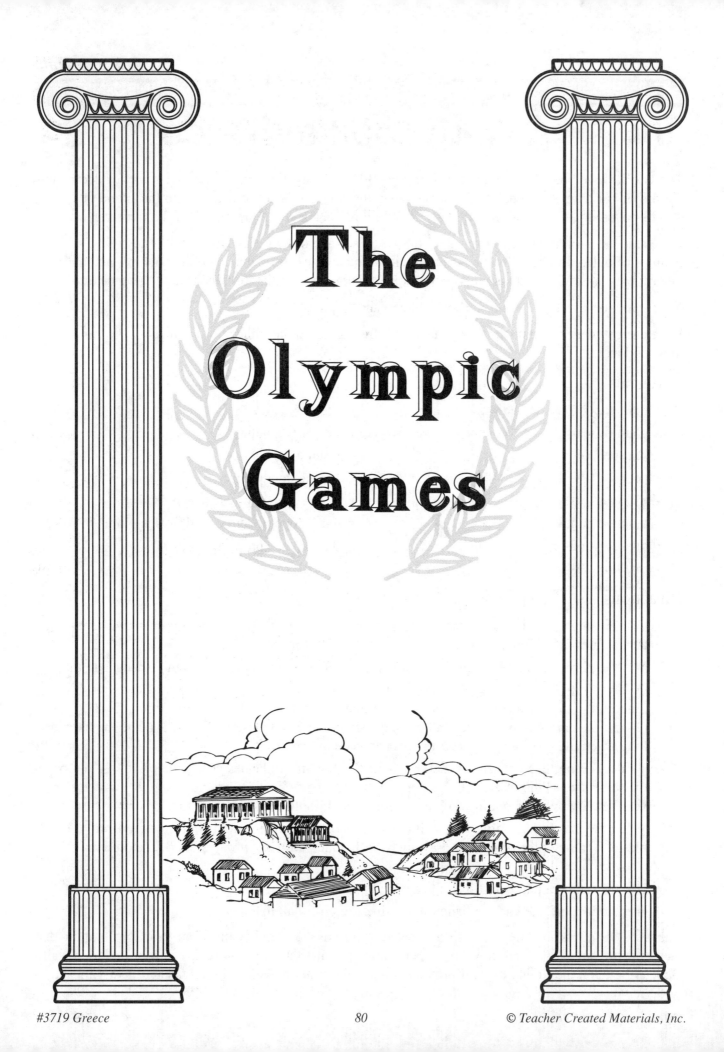

The Olympic Games

The Games That Belong to the World

The Olympic Games are sporting events that bring the whole world together in a sporting competition. Today, men and women participate in summer and winter games with many events. People from all over the world train for years to take part in these games. The Olympic Games began many years ago in Greece.

The first Olympic Games were held in Greece in the city-state of Elis. The site of the games was called Olympia. The first recorded date for the games was in 776 B.C., but the games probably began hundreds of years before that. They were held every four years and were so important that the Greek calendar was based on the four-year Olympiad.

The city-states of Greece were often at war with each other, but during the time of the Olympics, they would declare a truce so that athletes could travel safely to the site of the games. This was called the "Sacred Truce."

Only men could participate and attend the games. The early games were open to pure Greek men with no police record. There were other less important games in which women competed in running races.

The games were held in honor of Zeus. During the festivities the athletes, judges, and guests would make a procession to a great statue of Zeus and make a sacrifice of 100 oxen. The statue was made of gold and ivory and was one of the seven wonders of the ancient world.

Running was the only event in the original Olympics. Later, a pentathlon was added. *Pentathlon* means "five events" and included the broad jump, discus, javelin, wrestling, and the 200-yard (183-meter) dash. Even later, other events were added to the program including boxing and chariot racing.

Today, our athletes wear brightly colored uniforms that display the colors of their countries or other designs. In the original Olympic Games, the athletes competed without clothes at all. They would cover their bodies with olive oil. After the games they would scrape off the oil and sweat with a scraper called a *strigil*. The mixture of oil and sweat was considered to be magical and was saved in small bottles.

The last record of Olympic winners was made in 261 A.D., but no one is sure when the games actually ended. The Olympic games were reborn in 1896 in Athens, Greece.

The Games That Belong to the World *(cont.)*

The first modern Olympic games were held in Athens in 1896. There were 14 countries and 285 athletes who participated. The opening ceremony was scheduled to commemorate the seventy-fifth anniversary of the liberation of Greece. The modern Olympics were the dream of Baron Pierre de Coubertin.

The Baron studied Ancient Greece when he was in school and was impressed by the importance the games played in Greek culture. He proposed that the Olympics should be a way for countries to develop friendship and cooperation. He wanted the games to help bring people together for world peace and to help abolish racial discrimination. The International Olympic Committee was formed in 1894 with Dimitris Vikelas as its first president, and Pierre served as secretary general.

The tradition of the lighting of the Olympic flame started in 1936 at the opening ceremony in Berlin. The symbolic tie to the Greek games in Olympia was carried out by lighting the flame on the altar of the Temple of Hera. Girls dressed in ancient Grecian clothing surrounded their leader who acted as the priestess. Her torch was then lit from the rays of the sun by using a metallic reflector. The acting priestess placed the flame in a special vessel and passed it to a runner who carried it to the memorial of Baron Pierre de Coubertin. It was lit in his honor. Then the flame was taken by thousands of athletes to Athens. From there the flame was taken to the designated city where the games were to be held. The ceremony for the lighting of the flame continues to this day.

It was Coubertin's proposal that the games would be held every four years but in a different country each time. On page 86 is a list of places where the Olympic Games have been held. Locate each place on a map of the world. Which countries have hosted the Olympics more than once?

What do you think about the ideas that the Baron had? How do you think they have helped the world toward the goal of peace?

The Opening and Closing Ceremonies

The Opening Ceremony begins with the arrival of the head of state of the host country. The anthem of that country is played. Next, comes the parade of the officials and the competitors, wearing their team uniforms. The Greek team is always the first to enter and all others follow in alphabetical order. (The team from the host country is always last.)

Each team has someone who carries a sign to identify the team and another member is chosen by the coaches to represent the team by carrying the flag. It is a great honor to be selected for this privilege.

The teams vary in size from one individual to several hundred athletes. Which countries do you think have had the largest teams or the smallest? Why? Why don't some countries participate in the Winter Games?

Speeches are given by the president of the organizing committee of the host country. This person has worked for several years to prepare his city for this event. Why does it take so much time to prepare for hosting the Olympic Games? What has happened in the last two decades that have made it a tougher job?

A speech is given by the president of the IOC (International Olympic Committee). The last president was Juan Antonio Samaranch from Spain (1980–2001). The new president is Jacques Rogge from Belgium (2001–present). This is an important position that takes a lot of volunteer hours. There have been eight presidents since the beginning of the modern games.

Official words are read by a local representative: "I declare open the Olympic Games of _____ celebrating the Olympiad of the modern era."

The Olympic flag is brought into the arena while the Olympic hymm is played. A three-gun salute is fired, and doves of peace are released. The doves are an important symbol of the games. They are a sign of goodwill that shows that countries will try to forget their differences. In Atlanta, Georgia, in 1996, children made dove kites and others had paper doves on poles to remind the adults of the purpose of the Olympics. The whole world watches for two weeks as athletes represent their nations in a peaceful manner. Why was it important at the Atlanta games for people to be reminded of the peaceful intent of the Olympic Games? What event happened there that was not so peaceful?

The Opening and Closing Ceremonies *(cont.)*

Then, the Olympic torch is carried into the arena. The torch has made a long journey to get to this point with people of all ages and nationalities carrying it. The excitement mounts when the surprise athlete (usually from a past game) enters the stadium. There are still more surprises as he or she hands the torch off to several other athletes who proudly hold it up around the ring and finally race it to the final person who is to light the Olympic flame. In 1996 Mohammed Ali brought people to their feet as he raised the torch to light the flame that would burn throughout the games. Find out what other famous people have had the privilege to light the Olympic flame.

One of the judges and one of the athletes take the oath of fair play on behalf of the other participants.

Finally, a spectacular program of entertainment highlighting the host country's heritage and culture through music, artistic lighting, and costumes and dance is presented to the guests and the world. Visually, it speaks to every nation through the language of art.

At the last Winter Games in Salt Lake, Utah, almost 4.5 billion people watched the breath-taking opening ceremonies . . . this is about 85% of the planet. Many kids your age skated, sang, or took part in some way. The theme of the games was friendship, peace, and unity. Creatively woven throughout the program was a child skating and carrying a lantern. What do you think the lantern could represent?

At the closing ceremony, the athletes reunite and enter the stadium in no particular order. Hopefully, the athletes have made friends and this is a sign of the unity among nations. The national anthem of Greece is performed and its flag is raised along with the flag of the next host country. The mayor of the host city then presents the Olympic flag to the president of the IOC who in turn gives it to the mayor of the next host city. The president then declares the games closed and announces that they will assemble in four years at the next location to celebrate the next games.

The flame is extinguished, the Olympic hymn played, and the flag is lowered and taken horizontally out of the stadium.

All the athletes may not be at the closing ceremonies. Some have jobs, new babies, or other obligations, but those who do stay enjoy one last spectacle presented by their host city.

The Opening and Closing Ceremonies *(cont.)*

Extension Activity

The athletes enter the stadium in alphabetical order after the Greek team. But, whose alphabet does the list go by? The hosting country. So when the U.S. Olympic team is in Mexico, it is referred to as "los Estados Unidos de America," but in Australia, England, and other English speaking countries, the country is referred to as the "United States of America." In Germany the country is referred to as "Vereinigte Saaten von Amerika" and in France as "Etats-Unis."

In which country would the U.S. Olympic team enter the stadium earliest?

Here is a list of some of the countries that have participated in the Olympics games. Can you put them in alphabetical order?

Zimbabwe	Malaysia
Gabon	Tonga
Cameroon	Australia
Poland	Guam
Luxembourg	Venezuela
Great Britain	Paraguay
Malta	Barbados
Denmark	Jamaica
Albania	Chile
Qatar	Guatemala

Have you ever watched the parade of athletes?

Have you ever dreamed of being one of them? Write a little story about how you would feel if you were marching in the parade of athletes. Which sport would you want to represent? How would you feel marching in front of the whole world?

List of Olympic Games

Date	Location
1896	Athens, Greece
1900	Paris, France
1904	St. Louis, Missouri, USA
1908	London, England
1912	Stockholm, Sweden

The Olympic Games were cancelled in 1916 due to World War I

Date	Location
1920	Antwerp, Belgium

Separate winter Olympics first held in 1924.

(The Winter Games are listed first for each year.)

Date	Location
1924	Chamonix, France Paris, France
1928	St. Moritz, Switzerland Amsterdam, Netherlands
1932	Lake Placid, New York, USA Los Angeles, California, USA
1936	Garmisch-Partenkirchen, Germany Berlin, Germany

The Olympic Games were cancelled in 1940 and 1944 due to World War II.

Date	Location
1948	St. Moritz, Switzerland London, England
1952	Oslo, Norway Helsinki, Finland
1956	Cortina, Italy Melbourne, Australia
1960	Squaw Valley, California, USA Rome, Italy

Date	Location
1964	Innsbruck, Austria Tokyo, Japan
1968	Grenoble, France Mexico City, Mexico
1972	Sapporo, Japan Munich, Germany
1976	Innsbruck, Austria Montreal, Canada
1980	Lake Placid, New York, USA Moscow, Russia
1984	Sarajevo, Yugoslavia Los Angeles, California, USA
1988	Calgary, Canada Seoul, Korea
1992	Albertville, France Barcelona, Spain

Now, the summer and winter games are not held in the same years. They are on different four-year cycles so that there are Games every two years.

Date	Location
1994	Lillehammer, Norway (winter)
1996	Atlanta, Georgia, USA (summer)
1998	Nagano, Japan (winter)
2000	Sydney, Australia (summer)
2002	Salt Lake City, Utah, USA (winter)
2004	Athens, Greece (summer)
2006	Turin, Italy (winter)
2008	Beijing, China (summer)

Make an Olympic Flag

The flag of the Olympic Games is known throughout the world. It has five interconnected rings of blue, yellow, black, green, and red. At least one of the colors is present on the flag of every nation in the world.

The five rings represent the five continents that take part in the Olympic games: Asia and Europe (as one continent), North America, South America, Africa, and Australia.

Imagine that you have been asked to design a new Olympic flag. What colors would you use and what would your design look like? You can make your own Olympic flag to display.

Materials

- white paper or cloth
- markers, colored pencils, crayons
- paints and paintbrushes
- pencil
- *optional:* stencils, templates, etc.

Directions

1. Decide how large you want your flag to be and what colors you want to use.
2. On a piece of scratch paper, sketch a design in pencil of your new flag. Decide what shapes, symbols, pictures, etc., you want to use in your design.
3. Draw your completed design on the white paper or cloth and then color it in.
4. *Optional:* Add a frame or border around the completed flag.

A Motto for the Games

At the 1924 Olympics, the Olympic motto "Citius, Altius, and Fortius" was introduced in Latin.

The translation is "Faster, Higher, Braver." If you look at the Latin words, you can see that there are English words that are similar.

Citius

Citius is the Latin word meaning to set in motion. Our word excite comes from that root. If someone is excited, that person is usually in motion. Other words that come from that root are: *incite, resuscitate, solicitous*.

The Greek root for this word is *kinein* which means "to move." Also *kinetic*, which is anything that has to do with movement. Sometimes people claim to be able to move things by just thinking about them. That is called *telekinesis*.

Altius

When people talk about mountains, they measure how high they are by their *altitude.*

When planes are flying, they use an *altimeter* to measure how high they are.

Can you think of any other words that start with *alti* and mean "high"? Use the dictionary to see what you can discover.

Fortius

What words can you use in the following sentences? These words should start with *fort* and mean something strong.

- The soldiers remained in the _____ to defend it from the enemy.

- The man showed a lot of _____ by not giving in to smoking.

- The people used sandbags to _____ the walls of the city when the flood came.

By the way, the *fort* words are *fortress, fortitude,* and *fortify.*

Use a dictionary to make a list of words with these roots. Find the relationship between the words and the meanings of the roots.

Carrying the Flames of the Games

Carrying an Olympic torch is a great honor. Before each of the Olympic Games, a fire is lit that will burn during the entire games. The fire is a symbol that has been used since the beginning of the Olympic Games. At the original games, a flame was constantly kept burning in the altar to Zeus. The fire used at the modern games comes from a fire that is kept burning in Olympia, Greece, at the altar of Hera.

In order to get the fire from Greece to the site of the games, a torch is lit. The torch is carried in a relay from one runner to another until the fire is lit at the opening ceremonies of the games.

Each Olympic Games has its own torch design. The designs reflect the times and the tastes of the designers. Examine some of the torches that have been used through the years and discover how interesting the designs are. There are Websites that display the torch designs. The book *Olympics* is also a good resource.

This is your chance to design your own Olympic torch.

Materials

- 22" x 28" (56 cm x 71 cm) poster board
- scissors
- masking tape
- torch pattern on page 90
- construction paper or aluminum foil
- glitter
- flashlight

Directions

1. Begin at one corner and roll the poster board into a cone shape.

2. Leave the opening about 7" (18 cm) in diameter.

3. Tape the loose edge of the poster board and the tip of the cone to hold it in shape.

4. Decide how you want to design your torch and then cut the opening into the desired shape. You may want to investigate the torches of past Olympic Games to get ideas.

5. Cut the flames from red, orange, and yellow construction paper. Glue glitter around the edges of the flames. Attach the flames to the inside of the torch.

6. Put a flashlight inside the torch and use crumpled paper to hold it in place.

Here are some ideas:

- Cover your torch with aluminum foil or another shiny foil to make it look metallic.

- Cut the edge of the opening into a fancy design.

- Use the name of your city or school in the design.

- Replace the construction paper flames with colored tissue paper or plastic wrap crumpled into a flame shape and insert it into the top of the torch.

Carrying the Flames
of the Games *(cont.)*

90

Torch Relay Math

When the winter Olympic Games were held in Salt Lake City, Utah, in 2002, the Olympic torch was carried in a cross-country relay that covered 46 of the United States. The relay started in Atlanta where the last Olympic Games in the United States were held. Between December 4, 2001, and February 8, 2002, 11,500 runners carried the torch from Atlanta to Salt Lake City. Traditionally, the torch is carried for 1 kilometer (1,094 yards) by each runner when possible. The torch traveled by foot, plane, train, dogsled, snowmobile, and other means to get to its destination.

Here are some facts about the torch relay to Salt Lake City.

Total distance	more than 13,500 miles (21,726 km)
Participants	11,500
States	46
Days	65
Average distance per day	208 miles (335 km)
Time of relay each day	12 hours

Let's do some torch relay math!

1. The torch traveled an average of 208 miles (335 km) every day. It was carried for 12 hours a day. On the average, how many miles did it travel each hour?

2. The torch traveled a total of 13,500 miles (21,726 km). 11,500 people helped carry the torch. If each person had carried the torch for the same distance, how far would each person have carried the torch?

3. The torch traveled for 12 hours each day. The relay lasted for 65 days. How many hours did the torch travel all together?

4. The torch traveled through 46 states. How many of the states did the torch not travel through?

Hint: Fold this section under before reproducing.

Answers: 1. 17.33 miles (28 km)   **2.** 1.173 miles (1.89 km)   **3.** 780 hours   **4.** 4

The Discus

A discus is a flat, round disk which is thrown for distance. In Ancient Greece, the discus was made from stone, iron, bronze, or lead. The discus thrower was judged by his ability to throw the disk long distances. The Greeks also admired the rhythm and style used by the thrower. The weight of the discus varied. Boys usually used a lighter discus.

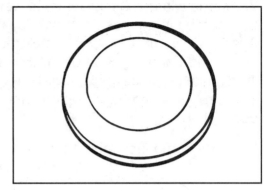

Today, the discus is still an Olympic event. The disks are made from wood with metal edges. The weight of the discus for men is 2 kilograms (4.4 lbs.). The weight of the discus for women is 1 kilogram (2.2 lbs.).

In the Olympics, the men and women compete separately. The record for men's discus was set on July 31, 1996, at the summer games in Atlanta, Georgia. The record setter was Lars Riedel, a German, who threw the discus 69.40 meters (75.89 yards or 227.70 ft.). The record for women's discus was set on September 29, 1988, by Martina Helman, a German, at Seoul, Korea. She threw the discus 72.40 meters (79.07 yards or 237.20 ft.). Why do you think the woman competitor could throw hers further than the man could?

You can have your own discus competition. Follow the directions on page 93 for making your discus.

To hold your competition you will need these items:

- a large open area either outside or in a gymnasium
- masking tape or chalk to mark the standing line
- a very long measuring tape
- a discus for each competitor
- a person to measure how far the discus is thrown
- a person to keep score
- a score sheet

How to throw your discus:

- Hold your arm straight by your side.
- Hold the discus in your hand so that it is under your arm.
- Turn quickly in a circle twice and let go of the discus.
- The person who is measuring should report to the scorekeeper how far the discus went when it first landed.

The scorekeeper writes the name of the thrower and how far the discus went on the score sheet. At the end of the competition, the person with the longest throw wins.

You many want to allow each thrower to throw his or her discus three times and take the best score.

Students should have a chance to practice before the competition.

Each student should have a discus of the same weight.

The Discus *(cont.)*

Directions for Making Your Discus

Here are three different ways to make your discus:

Put two round paper plates top to top. Staple them together around the outer edge and then decorate.

Use two 10" (25 cm) cardboard circles from a pizza box. Staple them together around the outer edges and decorate.

Cut two 10" (25 cm) cardboard circles, staple them together around the outer edge, and decorate.

After making your discus, follow these steps to design and use it.

Choose a symbol from Greek mythology to use in decorating your discus. Ancient competitors used pictures of Hercules or other strong heroes. You might choose a symbol that represents your interests or personality

Draw your choice of symbol on your discus and color it.

Practice throwing it in a straight line. It may be harder than it looks!

       #3719 Greece

Wreaths for the Winners

Winners of today's Olympic Games stand before the crowds and receive medals of gold, silver, and bronze. The winners of the ancient Olympic Games received leaves.

Crowns of olive leaves were the prize for winning the Olympic Games in Ancient Greece. The leaves were taken from a sacred olive tree that grew behind the temple of Zeus at Olympia. This was the greatest and most treasured prize that an athlete could win.

The Olympic games were not the only games in Ancient Greece. On the years when the Olympics were not held, there were three other national athletic competitions. These were called the "Panhellenic Games." *Panhellenic* means that they included athletes from every part of the country.

"The Nemean Games" honored Zeus, as did the Olympics, but at the Nemean Games, the grand prize was a bunch of wild celery! "The Pythian Games" honored Apollo and were held at Delphi. There the winners wore wreaths of laurel to show their status. "The Isthmian Games" honored Poseidon and were held in Corinth. The grand prize at that event was a wreath of pine. Later, these three competitions offered money to the athletes for prizes and for competing. The Olympic Games never did.

You can make a wreath to award the winners of your class Olympics.

Materials

- a length of ribbon long enough to go around someone's head
- individual leaves on separate wire stems often found in craft stores

Directions

Tightly wrap the wire stems around the ribbon at 1/2" (1.3 cm) intervals. Make sure that all of the leaves are going in the same direction. The backs of the leaves should be toward the person's head when the ribbon is tied, and all of the leaves should be going forward. Tie the ribbon around the winner's head and cheer!

Discussion Questions

- How do you feel about the prizes that the athletes won? Do you think you would work that hard to succeed if you were going to win a wreath?

- Have you ever won a trophy? How did that make you feel? Was it better than a wreath? Why?

- Who would come if your city hosted the Panamerican Games? Which countries would be involved? How many continents would be involved?

The Olive Wreath Award
for Good Sportsmanship

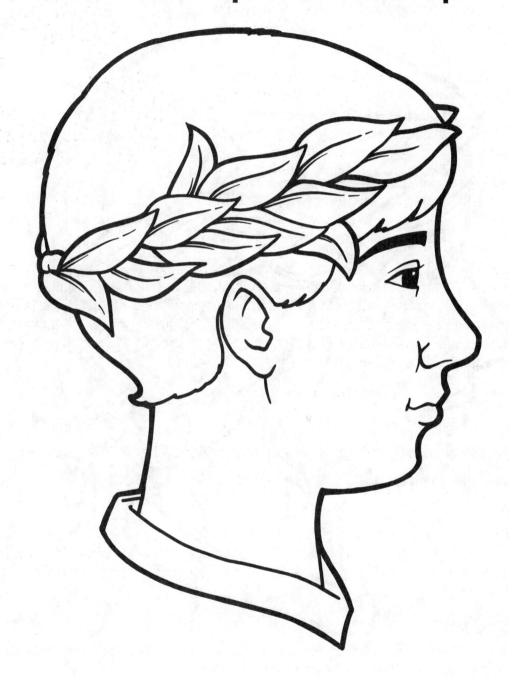

Awarded to _____

Date: _____

Achievement: _____

The Olive Wreath Award
for Good Sportsmanship *(cont.)*

Awarded to _____

Date: _____

Achievement: _____

96

Classroom Event Score Sheet

Use this scoring sheet for your own classroom event.

Name of Event:_____

Name	1st attempt score	2nd attempt score	3rd attempt score	Place in Event

The Olympic Scoreboard

As you watch the Olympic events, you can keep track of the nations that win the gold, silver, and bronze medals. Use the chart below to record in the winner of each medal.

EVENT	GOLD	SILVER	BRONZE

My Event Chart

You can use the chart below to keep a record of the events during the Olympic Games. Watch the event on television or get the results from another source and record the information in the correct areas below.

Name of Event _____

My Name _____

Athlete's name	Time or Distance of Attempt
Country	Place in Overall Event (Results)
Comment or other information	

Athlete's name	Time or Distance of Attempt
Country	Place in Overall Event (Results)
Comment or other information	

Athlete's name	Time or Distance of Attempt
Country	Place in Overall Event (Results)
Comment or other information	

Athlete's name	Time or Distance of Attempt
Country	Place in Overall Event (Results)
Comment or other information	

Making a Timeline

Timelines are used to show when things happened in history. A timeline shows events in chronological order. *Chronological* means in the order in which they happened.

You are going to practice making a timeline of your life.

Step #1: On page 101 list 10 important things that have happened to you in your life. Remember to list the date in which the event happened. If you do not remember the exact day, try to remember the month and year.

Step #2: Number the events in the order that they happened. Put a number "1" next to the first thing that happened, a "2" by the next thing, and so on until all the events are numbered. This is how you put things into chronological order.

Step #3: Glue or tape the 10 important events onto posterboard or butcher paper. Remember to keep them in chronological order. Write the date above the timeline and the event below the timeline.

Have you ever wondered . . .

- why would a timeline be useful to a reader?
- what types of events would be listed on a timeline?
- where would you find timelines?
- which subjects in school would be most likely to use timelines? Why?

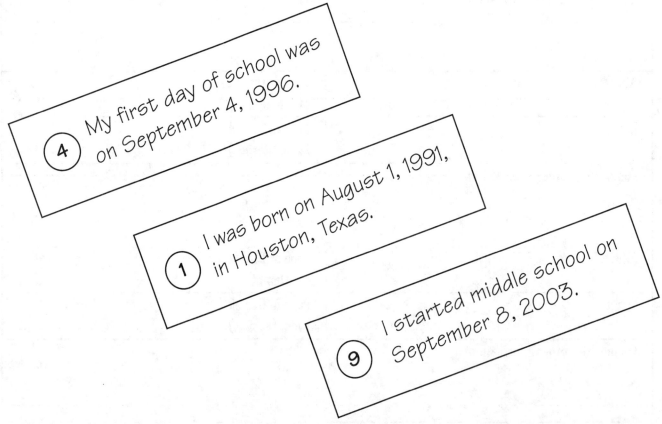

My Personal Timeline

Ten important things that have happened to me in my life.

Timeline Activities and Game

On the following pages is an Olympic history timeline game. Explain to your students what a timeline is and have them complete their personal timelines. After they have finished their timelines, have them discuss why they chose the events that they did for their timelines. Have them display their timelines. They might want to make larger ones on long sheets of paper.

Explain to the class that the Timeline Game is also a timeline, even though it is not straight. It presents key events in the history of the Olympic Games.

The game is a simple board game. Use buttons or beans for markers. Copy the pages of the game and tape them together to make a game board for each group of 4–6 players. Make a spinner to go with each game board. You may want the students to color their game boards and then laminate them for future use.

To determine the first player, each student spins the spinner. The one with the highest number starts. The student spins again and travels clockwise around the board. The students take turns spinning, moving, and following the directions on the board. The first student to reach the end wins. To make the end more challenging, you may require that the winner have the exact number he or she needs to reach the last space.

The purpose of the game is for students to learn some of the major events in Olympic history. Each student should be given a chance to finish the game even after the first player reaches the end.

An added challenge for the students: using a large world map, have the students locate each of the countries and cities which hosted the Olympics. Students can do this before the game begins or as they land on each new space.

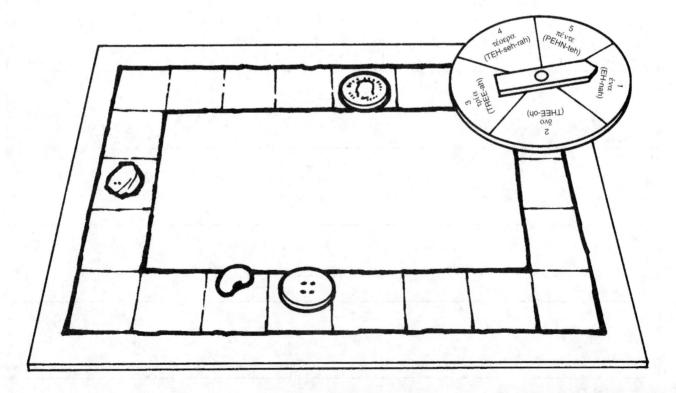

Timeline Spinner

Copy the spinner circle and arrow below and glue each to lightweight cardboard. Cut out the circle and the arrow. Punch a hole in the center of the circle and at the indicated spot on the arrow. Color the spinner with bright colors, but let the numbers show. Attach the arrow to the spinner with a brass paper fastener.

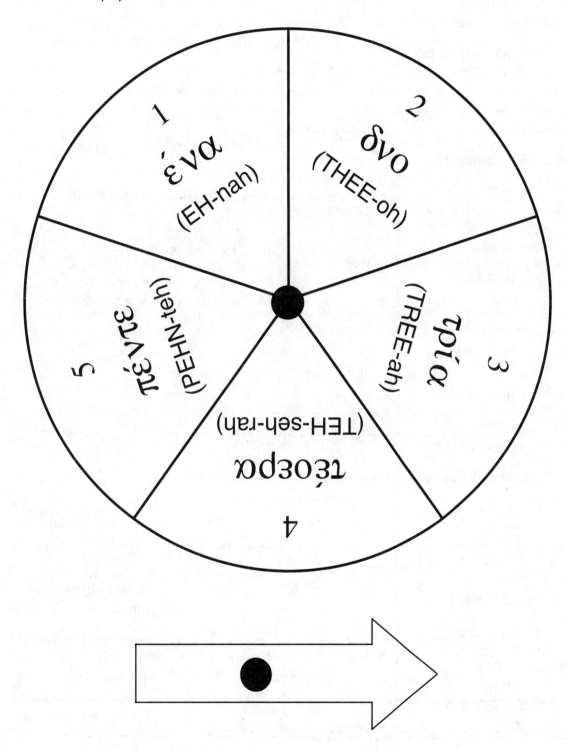

B

1908 – London, England

The Games were supposed to be held in Rome but were moved due to the eruption of Mt. Vesuvius.

Make a volcano noise and return to Start.

1904 – St. Louis, USA

There was little interest in the Games. The Americans won everything but the decathalon.

Count to ten.

1900 – Paris, France

American Ray Eway won 3 jumping events.

Jump forward 1 space.

↑ **You start here** ↑

The Olympic Games are revived by Pierre de Coubertin **1896 Athens, Greece**

Directions

- Cut this timeline section along the dashed lines.

- Attach it to another game section by matching the tabs.

- Glue the five sections to a large piece of construction paper.

E

1996 – Summer Atlanta, Georgia, USA

One hundred years of the modern Olympics was celebrated here. These were called the "Centenary Games."

A

**1928 – Winter
St. Moritz, Switzerland**

Sonja Henie was only 15 when she won a gold in figure skating.

Skate around the room.

Summer – Amsterdam, Netherlands

**1932 – Winter
Lake Placid,
New York, USA**

Summer – Los Angeles, California, USA

Mildred (Babe) Didrickson won gold in the javelin and 80 m (87.5 yards) hurdles.

Jump as high as you can!

**1936 – Winter
Garmisch-Partenkirchen, Germany**

Summer – Berlin, Germany

Jesse Owens set two Olympic and one world record in track events.

Stand up and cheer for Jesse!

C

1924 – Chamonix, France

This was the first separate Winter Games.

Summer – Paris, France

Johnny Weissmuller was the winning swimmer. He became famous as Tarzan in movies.

1920 – Antwerp, Belgium

This was the first time the Olympic flag was flown.

Wave to everyone playing this game.

1912 – Stockholm, Sweden

These were first Games to have women's swimming and the modern pentathlon.

"Swim" around the room.

B

Directions

- Cut this timeline section along the dashed lines.

- Attach it to another game section by matching the tabs.

- Glue the five sections to a large piece of construction paper.

The Olympic Games

C

The Olympic Games were cancelled in 1940 and 1944 because of World War II.

Go back 4 spaces.

1948
Winter –
St. Moritz, Switzerland

Summer –
London, England

1952
Winter – Oslo, Norway

Summer –
Helsinki, Finland

1956
Winter – Cortina, Italy
Summer – Melbourne, Australia
Equestiran events were held in Sweden.

Ride a horse.

1960
Winter –
Squaw Valley, California, USA
Summer – Rome, Italy

1964
Winter –
Innsbruck, Austria
Summer – Tokyo, Japan

1968
Winter – Grenoble, France
Summer – Mexico City, Mexico
Enriqueta Basilio was the first woman to light the Olympic flame.

Move ahead 2 spaces.

1972
Winter – Sapparo, Japan
Summer –
Munich, Germany
A terrorist attack against the Israeli team killed 17 people.

Go back 4 spaces.

D

Directions

- Cut this timeline section along the dashed lines.

- Attach it to another game section by matching the tabs.

- Glue the five sections to a large piece of construction paper.

Directions

- Cut this timeline section along the dashed lines.

- Attach it to another game section by matching the tabs.

- Glue the five sections to a large piece of construction paper.

D

1976

Winter – Innsbruck, Austria

Summer – Montreal, Canada

Nodia Comaneci of Romania won 3 gold medals at age 14. She was the first gymnast to earn a perfect score of 10.

1980

Winter – Lake Placid, New York, USA

The USA hockey team wins an unexpected victory!

Summer – Moscow, Russia

The USA and 64 other countries boycott.

Go back 4 spaces.

1984

Winter – Sarajevo, Yugoslavia

Summer – Los Angeles, California, USA

Carl Lewis won 4 golds in track events and tied Jesse Owens' record.

Run ahead 3 spaces

A

1994

Winter – Lillehammer, Norway

This was the first year that split up the summer and winter games.

1992

Winter – Albertville, France

Summer – Barcelona, Spain

This was the first year for freestyle skiing.

Ski around the room.

1988

Winter – Calgary, Canada

Summer – Seoul, Korea

This was the first time for both of these countries to host the Olympics.

Give a big cheer!

**2004 – Summer
Athens, Greece**

You Win!

Get your medal!

**2002 – Winter
Salt Lake City,
Utah, USA**

This was the first year
for women's bobsledding.
The surprise winners were
the USA team of Jill Bakken
and Vonetta Flowers.

**2000 – Summer
Sydney, Australia**

Marion Jones became
the first woman to win
5 medals in the
same Olympics.

Run to the finish!

**1998 – Winter
Nagano, Japan**

Three new sports
were introduced – women's
ice hockey, curling, and
snowboarding.

**Oops! You slipped off
your snowboard.
Go back 1 space.**

E

Directions

- Cut this timeline section along the dashed lines.

- Attach it to another game section by matching the tabs.

- Glue the five sections to a large piece of construction paper.

A Very Long Race

Have you ever seen a marathon? Many cities hold marathon races. In a marathon, people run more than 26 miles. They often run just for the challenge or the thrill of taking part in a big running event. Sometimes they run for large prizes. People who run in marathons often train for many years and run almost every day to prepare for the race. It is a great physical challenge for people to complete the course.

Why do we call these races "marathons"? There is a place in Greece named "Marathon." It is a plain northeast of Athens. In 490 B.C. Greece was threatened by invading Persians. A group of soldiers met the Persians on the plains of Marathon and fought them off. One soldier ran the 25 miles to Athens to report the victory. He shouted, "Rejoice, rejoice! We conquer!" Then he died.

In order to honor this brave runner, the modern Olympics of 1896 included a marathon race. The official distance of the race now is 26 miles 385 yards. Some marathons are now run at different lengths. There are often shorter races for people who cannot race the full 26 miles, but in South Africa the Comrades' Marathon is 52 miles long.

In the United States, several famous marathons are held each year. New York City, Boston and Chicago have important marathon races. Some cities have marathon races connected with other events. In Indianapolis there is a mini-marathon held before the Indianapolis 500 automobile race. Cities will also hold marathons for people who want to qualify for the bigger races in New York and Boston.

Activities

Make a list of some of the marathon races in the United States. Record any interesting information about the races.

Find out who the winners were for the most recent New York, Boston, and Chicago marathons. Compare their times. Which race seems to take longer to complete?

Many of the winners of the major marathons are from other countries. Find them on a world map.

If there is a marathon in your city, you may be able to volunteer to help out. Volunteer groups hand out water to the runners or help at the registration tables. See if there is a way you can help at one of the community runs in your area. Maybe your whole class can volunteer.

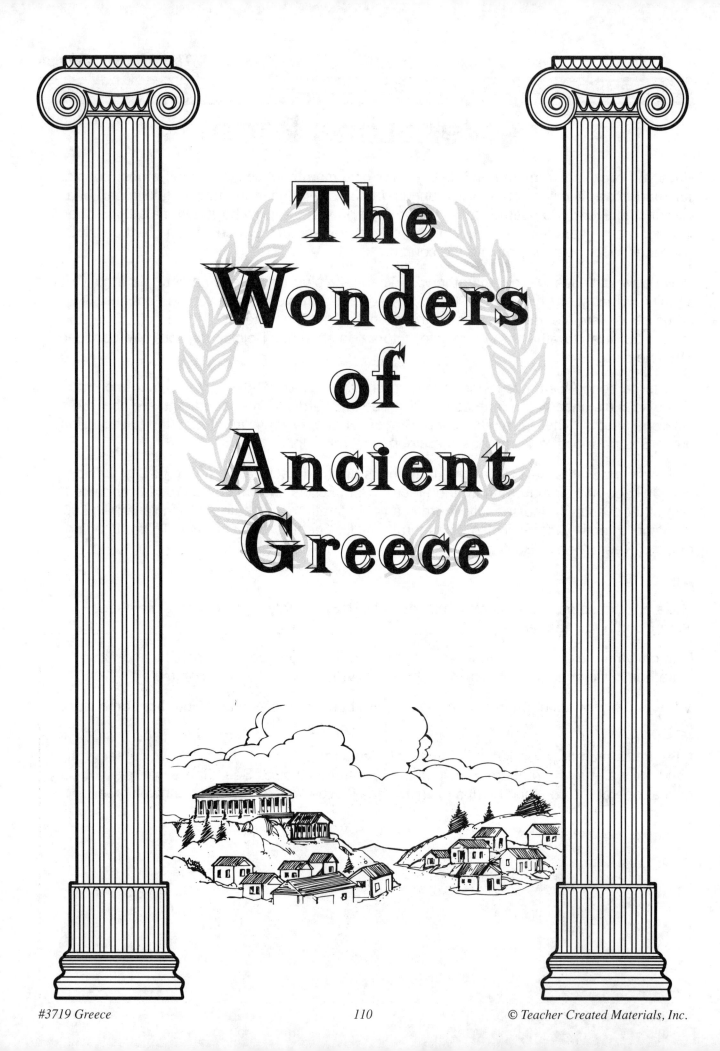

The Wonders of Ancient Greece

Alphabet Activities

The Greek alphabet is considered to be the origin of the major European alphabets in use today. It is fun for the students to examine and explore the development of our alphabet. These activities are designed to help your class learn about the Greek alphabet and how it influences our language even today.

Hand out the copy of the Greek alphabet on the page 112. Read through the alphabet with the children. There are several different ways to pronounce the Greek letters; this list displays the most common ways in ancient and modern Greek.

Use these discussion questions to help the students think more about the alphabet.

1. Where do you think the word *alphabet* originated? Look at the first two letters of the Greek alphabet.

2. Which of these letters have you seen before? Where?

3. Which letters of the Greek alphabet look the same as our letters in upper case?

4. Which letters are pronounced the same as our letters?

5. What letters do we have in our alphabet that the Greeks did not have in theirs? Why do you suppose those letters are missing? What do you think the Greeks did for the sound of "J" or "C"?

6. Which Greek letters are combinations of two of our letters? Do you think this is a useful idea? Why or why not? What letters could we combine in our alphabet to make a new letter? Can you design your own letter?

The Greek Alphabet

Here are the letters of the Greek alphabet. You can see how similar some of the letters are to the ones that we use. Practice pronouncing the names of the letters. Practice writing the upper and lower case forms of the letters. The letter *sigma* has two lower case forms.

Greek Letters	Name	Pronunciation	This is the way the letters are pronounced:
A α	Alpha	(al-fah)	f**a**ther
B β	Beta	(bay-tah)	**v**ery or **b**erry
Γ γ	Gamma	(gam-mah)	**y**ou or **g**et
Δ δ	Delta	(del-tah)	**th**ose or **d**o
E ε	Epsilon	(ep-si-lon)	p**e**t
Z ζ	Zeta	(zay-tah)	**z**oo
H η	Eta	(ay-tah)	h**ey**
Θ θ	Theta	(thay-tah)	**th**ing
I ι	Iota	(eye-o-tah)	h**i**gh
K κ	Kappa	(kap-pah)	**k**ind
Λ λ	Lambda	(lam-dah)	**l**ike
M μ	Mu	(mew)	**m**any
N ν	Nu	(new)	**n**one
Ξ ξ	Xi	(zie)	a**x**es
O o	Omicron	(oh-ma-kron)	b**o**x
Π π	Pi	(pie)	**p**ut
P ρ	Rho	(row)	**r**ose
Σ σ,ς	Sigma	(sig-mah)	**s**un
T τ	Tau	(tah)	**t**on
Y υ	Upsilon	(ee-psee-lon)	p**u**t
Φ φ	Phi	(fie)	**f**un
X χ	Chi	(kie)	boo**k**/lo**ch**
Ψ ψ	Psi	(sigh)	ma**ps**
Ω ω	Omega	(o-meh-ga)	b**o**x

112

Alphabet Search

Divide the class into teams of two or three students. Assign each team two or three letters of the Greek alphabet. Have them use the white pages of the telephone book to look up names of businesses that use Greek letter names. Have the students keep a record of their discoveries.

After the groups are finished, compare the results of each group. Discuss how many businesses use the word *alpha* in their name as compared to *lambda* or other letters. Look at the frequency of the other letters. Have students come up with reasons why people would choose to use Greek letters in the names of their businesses. Explain to them that using such as *nu* for *new,* for example, is different than using the Greek letter itself.

Also explain how *delta* might refer to geography and how this geographic feature got its name from the shape of the Greek letter.

Have the students make a chart of their results. A chart on large paper could be displayed in the school hallway for the rest of the school to observe. The chart may also be used as part of the final project for this unit.

Describe some common uses for Greek letters in our society. Tell them about Greek organizations that are social, professional, or academic.

You may want to tell the students about the uses of Greek letters in mathematics:

- pi = 3.14 the ratio of the circumference to the diameter of a circle
- Other uses of Greek letters are probably too advanced at this stage, but *sigma* and *chi* are used, along with others in advanced mathematics.
- *Alpha* and *omega* are often used to signify the beginning and ending of things.

On the following page is an activity that uses the Greek alphabet as a type of code. Have the students determine which English words have been written using the Greek alphabet. Have them write the translations on the lines provided.

Secret Messages:
A Greek Code Mystery

Demetrius and Anna heard that there were ancient Greek coins buried on an island in Greece. They decided to explore and find the treasure. They know that the treasure is in the Cyclades Islands in Greece, but they have to translate the names of the islands to find the one that is the farthest south.

Help the children find the treasure by translating the names of these Greek islands into English. When you are finished, follow the directions to find out which island has the treasure.

1. ΑΝΔΡΟΣ _____

2. ΣΕΡΙΦΟΣ _____

3. ΣΙΦΝΟΣ _____

4. ΜΙΛΟΣ _____

5. ΙΟΣ _____

6. ΘΙΡΑ _____

7. ΑΜΟΡΓΟΣ _____

8. ΜΙΚΟΝΟΣ _____

9. ΣΙΡΟΣ _____

10. ΚΕΑ _____

Now that you have named the islands, find them on a map of Greece. Find the island that is the farthest south.

Name the island where the treasure is buried: _____

- -

Hint: Fold this section under before reproducing.

Answers: **1.** Andros **2.** Serifos **3.** Sifnos **4.** Milos **5.** Ios **6.** Thira **7.** Amorgos **8.** Mykonos **9.** Syros **10.** Kea The answer is: Thira

Ancient Greek Coins

The Greeks used three main coins in their monetary system: *drachma*, the *stater*, and the *obol*. Each city-state would mint its own coins, so the designs on the coins would be different.

In Athens the drachma had a picture of Athena on one side and a picture of her owl on the reverse. These coins were called "owls."

Alexander the Great had silver drachma minted when he was in control of Greece. On one side was a picture of Zeus on his throne, and on the other side was a picture of Hercules that looked amazingly like Alexander himself. Alexander admired the two powerful role models.

Below are pictures of these two coins. The front of a coin is called the *obverse*. This is called "heads." The other side of a coin is called the *reverse* often referred to as "tails."

Note to Teachers: Copy this on tag board or heavier cardboard and have the students cut out and paste the coins together. You may want to have students make several of each coin to use in the marketplace or at the Olympics activity.

Drachma

Ancient Greek Coins *(cont.)*

Here are patterns for making two more Greek coins—*obols* and *staters*. The class can use these to make money for the Greek market and the Olympics.

Use the Ancient Greek Money Math acitivity on page 117. Have the students practice making change with the coins that they make.

Obol

Stater

Ancient Greek Money Math

The ancient Greeks used three main coins in their monetary system. These were the *drachma*, the *stater,* and the *obol.* The drachma was worth 6 obols. The stater was worth 2 drachma.

Using this information, answer the following questions.

1. Two drachma would equal _____ obols.

2. One stater would equal _____ obols.

3. One drachma is equal to _____ stater.

4. 24 obols is equal to _____ drachmas or staters.

Complete this chart by writing the names of the appropriate coins.

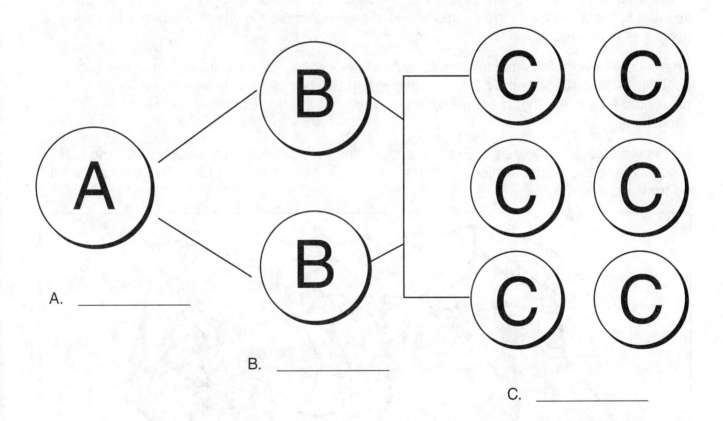

A. _____

B. _____

C. _____

Hint: Fold this section under before reproducing.

Answers: 1. 12   **2.** 12   **3.** 1/2   **4.** 4, 2

  A. stater   **B.** drachma   **C.** obol

Greek Drama

Have you ever seen a play? Have you ever been in one?

Plays are fun to watch and to be in. The ancient Greeks thought so, too. Drama as we know it today started in Ancient Greece.

The first plays were part of religious ceremonies. During the festivals to the god Dionysus, people would act out plays to honor the god and to entertain the people.

Greek plays included comedies and tragedies. Comedies were not necessarily funny. They were about average, everyday people who had good things happen to them at the end of the play. Tragedies were about upper class people who had bad things happen to them. In other words, plays that ended happily were considered to be comedies. Plays that ended badly were tragedies.

In Greek plays there was usually a chorus. A chorus could be one person or a small group of people who told the audience what was going on in the play. They would speak or sing an introduction and other parts of the play to keep the audience on track. There was not much scenery in these plays, so the chorus would sometimes describe where the play was taking place.

There were several famous playwrights in Ancient Greece. At the festivals, there would be contests to see who was the best. Aeschylus and Sophocles usually won when they presented plays. Another great playwright of classical Athens, Euripides, also won occasionally.

Masks were commonly used in Greek dramas. The actors would use masks portraying their emotions and their personalities. Some masks would be smiling and funny while others would be frowning and grim.

Greek Drama *(cont.)*

Put on a Classroom Drama

Hermes, Lord of Robbers was translated and adapted by Penelope Proddow and illustrated by Caldecott Award winner Barbara Cooney. It is a translation of one of the Homeric Hymns. These stories were used as introductions to longer stories by the Greek minstrels. The story is about the mischievous adventures of Hermes.

The story can be read to the class, or the class can read the poem in parts. It can be used to introduce the idea of a chorus in Greek drama.

Assign parts to the students. These are characters in the poem:

- Maia, the mother of Hermes

- Hermes, the mischievous god

- Apollo, the half-brother of Hermes, and god of archery, healing, music

- Ancient One, an old man

- Zeus, the father of Hermes and Apollo, king of the gods

The main characters will read the parts that are direct quotations by their characters.

Divide the other students into groups of three to five students to be the chorus. Have them read the parts that are not direct quotations by the main characters. Each chorus group can read a page, then trade. They should practice reading in unison.

Have the students make costumes and masks to do the play. The play can be used as part of the culminating activity for the Greek unit.

Students can use other myths to write plays of their own. Have them examine some of the myths and decide what could be read by the chorus and what could be read by individual actors.

Greek Masks

Masks played an important part in the Greek theater. They were used to show specific emotions like fear, sadness, happiness, laughter, and surprise. They were also used to portray a certain character, like an old man or a young woman. The features in the mask were exaggerated and often grotesque. There were even special masks for supernatural characters.

The masks covered the actor's entire head and were only worn by men, since women were not allowed on the stage. They were made from lightweight materials such as cork, leather, stiffened linen, and papier-mache. Human or animal hair was often added for a lifelike appearance. The actor had two holes for his eyes, but the masks were probably not very comfortable.

Pretending to be someone else can be a lot of fun. You can write your own play or try one based on one of Aesop's fables. You can use a mask to act out *Hermes, Lord of Robbers*.

Masks can be made from the Greek designs on the following pages or from new ones that you create.

Materials

paper plates, markers or crayons, string or elastic to keep the mask on

Directions

1. Draw your own mask and color it or cut out the masks on the following pages and glue them to the plates.
2. Cut out the eye holes.
3. Attach the string by placing holes on each side above your ears (not too close to the edge of the plate).
4. Add the string or elastic. Try it on for size.

   Optional: More masks can be made from papier-mache.

Discussion Questions

1. At Halloween many people like to wear masks. Can you think of some famous characters that people like to pretend to be?
2. What problems might an actor have had when he wore the masks?

Hint: Fold this section under before reproducing.

Answer: 1. Spiderman, Frankenstein, Casper, Superman, Mickey Mouse are some suggested answers.

   2. getting hot, trouble with breathing, not reciting his lines loudly enough, not being able to see well

Greek Masks *(cont.)*

Greek Masks *(cont.)*

Greek Masks *(cont.)*

Greek Fashion Statements

Greek clothing was very simple and loose. It suited the warm climate of the Greek islands and was made from materials that were easy to obtain.

Most clothing was made from linen or wool. The clothing was usually fashioned from pieces of fabric wrapped around the body, then pinned or belted into place. The fabrics were often dyed rich colors and sometimes decorated to represent the city-state in which one lived. Clothing was usually made by women, girls, and female slaves in the families.

The men usually wore knee-length tunics and leather sandals. They would use wool blankets or capes to keep warm when needed. Men wore longer tunics for more formal occasions. Their legs were bare, but they wore leather sandals.

The women wore several types of dress. They would pin the clothing at the shoulder and tie it around the waist with cords. Women enjoyed beautiful jewelry, especially dangling earrings, bracelets, and necklaces. Rich families wore jewelry of silver and gold.

Elaborate hairstyles were very popular. Women would wear their hair long, and braid it with colorful ribbons and headbands. Scented waxes and lotions held these carefully designed hairstyles in place.

Children wore short, loose garments that allowed them to move about freely. The same type of clothing was worn by slaves who had to move about to do chores and housework.

To keep the bright sun out of their faces while traveling, people (usually men) would wear a *petasos*. This hat had a broad brim to shade the face.

On the following pages are pictures and descriptions of some of the popular types of clothing worn by ancient Greeks.

124

Greek Clothing

Chiton—The chiton is a simple garment. It consists of two rectangular pieces of fabric sewn up the sides, leaving room for the arms, and joined at the shoulders. A belt tied around the waist completes the costume. This garment was worn by both men and women and could be either floor length or knee length.

Exomis—The exomis was worn by men. This garment was made from a length of fabric joined over one shoulder. The other shoulder was left bare. The exomis was tied at the waist, and the material was arranged to fall evenly from the belt. This could be knee-length or shorter.

Tunic—The tunic was a garment with a little more shape. The fabric was cut into a "T" shape and sewn along the sides and shoulders, leaving the neck and the armholes open. The tunic was tied at the waist. This was usually worn by men, often with an added cape.

Himation—This is the garment that later became known as the "Roman toga." The himation consisted of a long piece of fabric with no sewing. One end of the fabric was thrown over the left shoulder, and the rest of the fabric was wrapped around the body under the arms, and again over the shoulder. Sometimes the fabric would have weights attached to hold the ends in place.

Peplos—Peplos were worn by women, and there were two versions of this garment. A peplos is similar to a chiton, except that the top of the peplos is folded over to make a draped top. The two rectangular pieces are sewn up the sides, leaving room for the arms, then folded over toward the outside and joined at the shoulder with pins or fasteners. The garment is tied at the waist with a belt. A Doric peplos has a fold over the top that comes to the waist level. An Ionic peplos has a longer fold over the top which is tied under the belt and then bloused.

Let's Play "Ancient Greek Dress-Up!"

It is easy to create costumes like the ones that the ancient Greeks wore. Greece can be a very warm place during the summers, so their clothing was loose and simple. Most of these costumes can be made with twin bed sheets.

Read the descriptions of the Greek clothing on page 125. Then examine these diagrams to help you create your own look.

Chiton	**Exomis**
Tunic	**Himation**
Doric Peplos	**Ionic Peplos**

Pillars of the Past and Present

The Greeks were great architects. They designed and built beautiful and functional buildings. Many of their buildings are still standing after more than 2,000 years.

One of the most famous of the ancient Greek buildings is the Parthenon. When you see pictures of the Parthenon, you will see that it is made up of many pillars.

Pillars were important to Greek architecture. They used three types of columns that are still in use today:

Doric—a pillar that does not have much decoration at the top.

Ionic—a pillar that has a fancier top; at the top of an Ionic column is scrollwork. The edges of the top look like the rolled ends of a scroll.

Corinthian—the fanciest pillar of the three; the top of a Corinthian pillar is decorated with leaves and scrollwork.

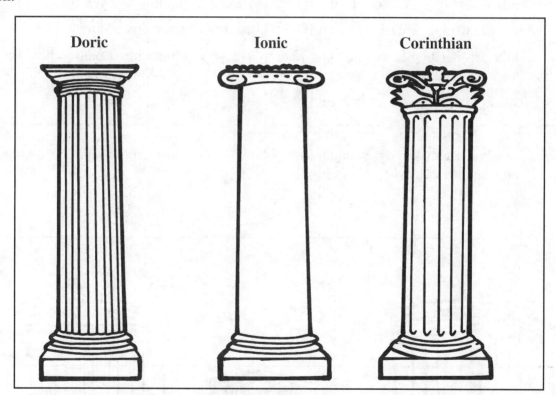

Doric   Ionic   Corinthian

Activity – Architectural Acavenger Hunt

Online: Find examples of the three types of columns used in buildings in cities in the United States and around the world. Look in Washington, D.C., Chicago, New York, London, Paris, Rome, and other cities.

In your own town: Look around in your own town to find buildings with these column types. Divide your class into teams and have a contest to see which team can find the most examples in 24 hours.

Travel to a different city: Maybe there is a city or town near you that you can explore. Some towns are known for their unusual architecture. Call ahead to the Chamber of Commerce and get a list of famous buildings. See if there is a walking tour available.

Design a Greek Building

On the following pages are illustrations of columns and architectural trims used in Greek architecture.

Copy these pictures and have the students create Greek buildings.

Materials

- boxes of various sizes (not too big)
- plain paper to cover the boxes – white or tan
- copies of the pictures on the next pages in various sizes
- tape
- glue
- markers

Directions

1. Look at pictures of buildings like the Parthenon or other Greek structures. Decide which building you would like to copy. Choose a box to fit the size of the building that you want to make.

2. If the box has writing or designs, cover it with plain paper before proceeding.

3. Cut out the architectural details that you want to use on your building. Decide where you want to place them, then glue them into place.

4. Use markers to draw any other features.

5. You can cut out doors or spaces between columns.

6. *Optional:* You can make larger buildings by following these instructions and drawing the columns and details on the sides of larger boxes.

Design a Greek Building *(cont.)*

Greek Ornaments

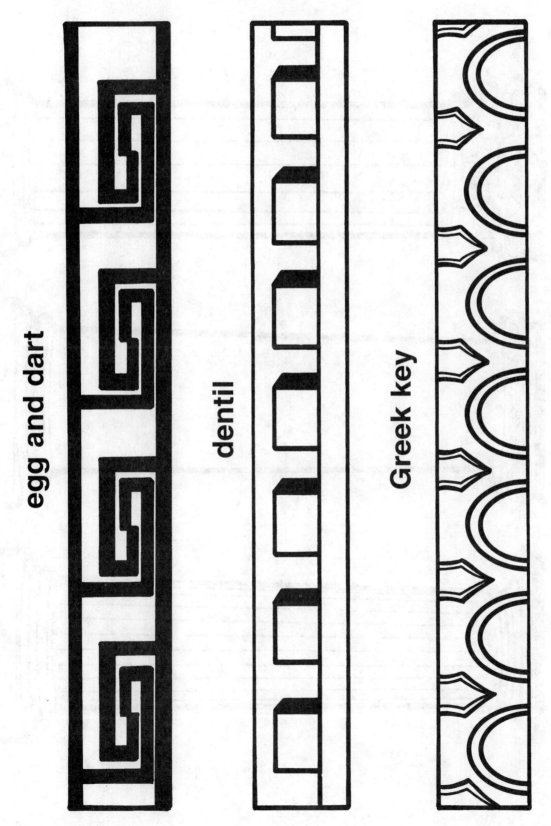

egg and dart

dentil

Greek key

Design a Greek Building *(cont.)*

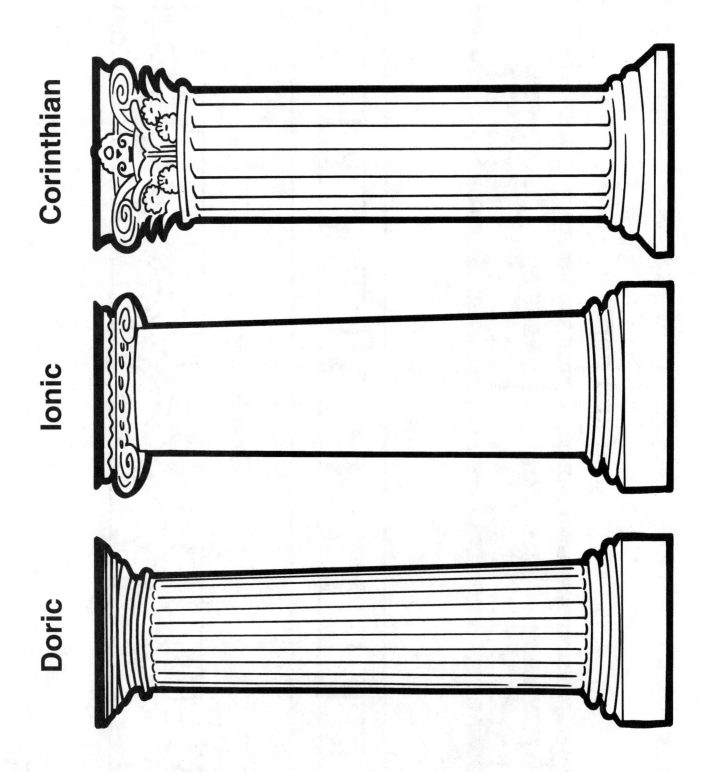

Corinthian

Ionic

Doric

Trojan Horse Teamwork Puzzle

This activity gives students the opportunity to discover how teamwork can be used for problem solving and critical thinking skills.

Duplicate the picture below and then follow these steps:

1. Cut the duplicated picture into quarters.
2. Copy each quarter at 200% or larger.
3. Cut each duplicated quarter into quarters and duplicate each piece again at 200% or larger.
4. Hand out the 16 pieces to the class or team. Have the students color the pieces any way that they would like to.
5. Have the students reassemble the 16 pieces into a large, colorful mural to display for the rest of the school.

Variations

1. You may choose to show them the picture before they attempt to solve it, or you may keep the finished picture a surprise.
2. You can duplicate the 16 pieces and keep dividing and enlarging to make a larger and more complicated finished project.
3. You may want to have the students stick to a color scheme rather than randomly coloring their individual pieces.

The Trojan Horse was a ruse designed by Odysseus and used by the Greeks in the Trojan War. Greek soldiers pretended to sail away from Troy, leaving behind a large, wooden horse as a present to the Trojans. The Trojans unsuspectingly rolled the large horse into the city and spent the night celebrating their victory. When the Trojans were asleep, Greek soldiers who were hiding inside the horse sneaked out and opened the gates of the city to admit the rest of the Greek army. The Greeks conquered Troy, and we acquired the expression, "Beware of Greeks bearing gifts." The story is told by Homer in *The Illiad*.

What Could These Be?

Teacher Note: Copy the next page and distribute to the class. Have the students guess what each object was used for. They can write their guesses in the blanks.

To make the exercises more challenging, do not give the students the answers and let them make their guesses without choices.

Students may work alone or with a team.

Students can take the worksheet home and ask other people for input.

There are hints included here to give to the students if they need them.

Answers (with hints)

1.	G	discus	This round disc was thrown by athletes in an Olympic event.
2.	L	weight	This was used by athletes to help them gain distance in a long jump.
3.	B	rattle	A rattle shaped like a pig with a nose-shaped handle.
4.	I	shoe	Most Greeks wore sandals.
5.	M	spindle	These spindles were used for spinning thread from wool.
6.	E	lamp	These small oil lamps were very common in Greece.
7.	C	perfume bottle	This perfume bottle is shaped like a foot with a sandal.
8.	F	bracelet	The snake bracelet was a very popular design with Greeks.
9.	H	scraper	Also called a *strigil,* this was used by athletes to scrape oil, dirt, and sweat from their bodies.
10.	J	top	Tops were popular children's toys.
11.	A	abacus	This type of counting frame was the calculator of Ancient Greece.
12.	N	protection charm	This amulet protected its owner from the evil eye.

What Could These Be? *(cont.)*

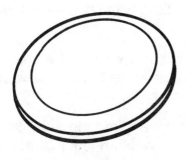

1. _____

2. _____

3. _____

4. _____

5. _____

6. _____

7. _____

8. _____

9. _____

10. _____

11. _____

12. _____

The Spartans

How would you like to join the army at age seven? In parts of Ancient Greece, that was what was expected of young boys.

Laconia was a city-state of Greece. Its capital city was Sparta. Laconia was famous for having a strict military lifestyle for its citizens. The most important activities in Laconia were the building of an army and teaching its members how to fight.

Spartan people lived by very strict guidelines. When the young boys entered the army, they were given only one piece of clothing to wear and no shoes. They went barefoot in the summer and the winter. They ate only very simple food and slept in rough barracks. They were expected to grow up and be fearless warriors for the city-state.

The young girls lived simple lives, too. They were taught to prepare food and keep a nice house. Their goal in life was to marry a solider and have a big family of healthy boys who would grow up to be soldiers.

Today, we use the word *spartan* to mean something without decoration or frills. If a person lives a spartan lifestyle, it means that they live simply and do not buy anything extra or unnecessary. They might have a very plain house or wear very plain clothing.

The people of Laconia were also encouraged to speak very little. They tried to say what they needed to say in very few words. Today, we use the word *laconic* to mean "using few words." If someone is laconic, then that person does not say much, or remains quiet around other people.

Activities

- Make a list of the things that you think you need to have in your life.

- Make another list of the things that you have that you would be willing to give up in order to live a spartan lifestyle.

- Pretend you are a child living in Laconia. Write a story about one day in your life. You may want to look at some pictures before you begin.

Creating a Historical Greek Mural (Class Project)

Creating a class mural is a great way to teach about the history of Greece and also a great way to demonstrate what the class has learned. This project can be used to promote research and teamwork. It is also a good way to decorate a school hallway, lunchroom, or classroom.

Divide the class into small groups. Assign each group a period of history to study. These are some ideas:

Minoan Civilization B.C. 200–1500

Mycenaean Culture in Greece B.C. 1500–1100

Trojan Wars ca. B.C. 1250

Dark Ages begin ca. B.C. 1100–800

Olympic Games begin ca. B.C. 776

Classical period from B.C. 480 to 323

Hellenistic Age B.C. 323–30

Wars between the Persians and the Greeks B.C. 499–478

Building of the Parthenon ca. B.C. 448–432

Reign of Alexander the Great B.C. 336–323

Greece becomes part of the Roman Empire B.C. 30

Choose as many or as few of these as you need for your class. You may want to make a mural that deals only with one topic, such as the "Olympic Games." Have students look for artwork that relates to the topic they are studying. Have them take a look at the murals that have been discovered on the buildings and pottery uncovered by recent archeological teams.

Materials

- sheets of paper 5–6 feet long for each group
- pencils
- markers or colored chalk (pastels)

- paint
- brushes
- small aluminum pie pans for mixing paints

Creating a Historical Greek Mural
(Class Project) *(cont.)*

Directions

Have the team decide which pictures they are going to use on their mural, and have them make a rough draft on smaller paper. Stress to them that everyone should have a chance to draw part of the picture. Also stress that planning is important so that the team can include everything that they want to in the mural. Planning is also important because making a mural is a large project, and it is best to not have to spend too much time with large murals spread out on the classroom floor. When students begin the actual painting, it is good to set aside a whole morning or afternoon for this activity.

Have the teams lightly sketch their work onto the paper with a pencil.

The mural can be as complicated or as simple as you choose, depending upon the ages and abilities of the students. With younger children, you may want to use pencils and markers. With older children, you may choose to use colored chalk, pastels, or paints.

Using paints allows students to learn about colors by mixing the paints to get new colors. Students should only mix small amounts of paints at a time in aluminum plates or other small dishes.

It is important to have good paint brushes for the children to use, as old, over-used ones tend to frustrate children who are trying to paint within the lines of their pictures. Teach the children that it is important to wash out and care for their brushes at the end of each painting session.

Whether students are using paints, chalks, markers, or pencils, it is best to begin with the lighter colors and work toward the darker ones. Students should wear old shirts or aprons when working on the murals.

It is possible to have the murals sponsored by a special interest group. This teaches students about the value of sponsoring the arts in a community. The students may be able to solicit funds for their murals before they begin the projects. Parent groups, public broadcasting groups, and community businesses might be interested in sponsoring a mural. Have a formal unveiling along with your Olympic Games or Agora as part of your culminating activity.

The Greeks were great patrons of the arts, and art sponsorship was a large part of the Greek culture.

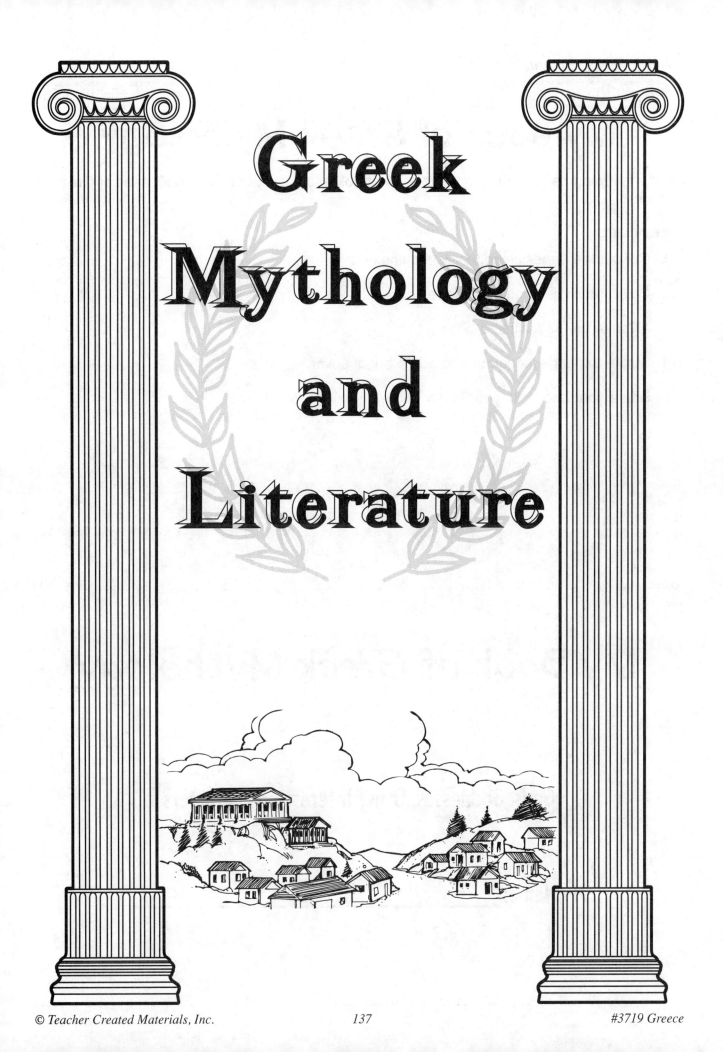

Greek Mythology and Literature

My Book of Greek Mythology

On the following pages, you can make a little book about the gods and goddesses of Greek mythology.

Directions

1. Cut out the pages along the dotted lines.

2. Color the pictures on each page.

3. Arrange the pages into a book.

4. Staple the pages together and add a bright cover.

5. Share your book with your family and friends.

- -

My Book of Greek Mythology

Gods, Goddesses, Other Interesting Characters

My Name: _____

- -

My Book of Greek Mythology (cont.)

Olympus

Mt. Olympus is the highest mountain in Greece. The top of it is always covered with clouds.

It was believed to be the home of the gods and goddesses. They sat on the mountain and watched the people on earth.

Ambrosia

Ambrosia was the food of the gods on Mt. Olympus. This wonderful food was only available to the gods, and it was said to be very delicious. The drink of the gods was called "nectar."

My Book of Greek Mythology *(cont.)*

Gaea

She was the mother of the Titans, Cyclopes, furies, giants, and tree nymphs, and, she was the goddess of the earth, marriage, and death. Her name is the root for our word "geography."

Uranus

He was the father of the first gods. He was the son and husband of Gaea. He was overthrown by Zeus. The planet Uranus is the seventh planet from the sun in our solar system. It is the only one named for a Greek god.

My Book of Greek Mythology *(cont.)*

Titans

These were the 12 children of Uranus and Gaea. They were the first gods, but were overthrown by Zeus and the other Olympians. Their names were Oceanus, Creus, Coeus, Iapetus, Cronus, Hyperion, Rhea, Mnemosyne, Theia, Themis, Tetys, and Phoebe. The ship *Titanic* was named for these gods because it was so large.

Cronus and Rhea

Cronus and Rhea were Titans and were the parents of Zeus. Cronus was the youngest Titan and was the god of fate and agriculture. Cronus is the root of our word chronology which means "time ordered." Other words having to do with time have the same root.

My Book of Greek Mythology (cont.)

Zeus

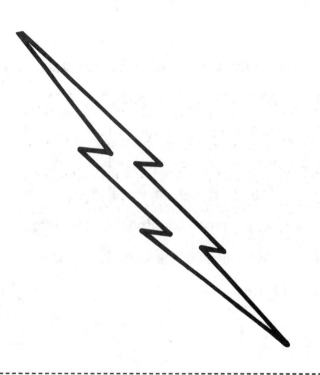

Zeus was the father of the Olympian gods and mortals. He was the master of destiny, god of the sky and weather. He had 140 children including Herakles and other heroes. He gained his power by overthrowing the Titans.

Hera

She was the most important of the goddesses. She was the wife of Zeus and the queen of heaven. She was the protector of all women. She was the queen of intriguers and was always tricking Zeus.

142

My Book of Greek Mythology *(cont.)*

Apollo

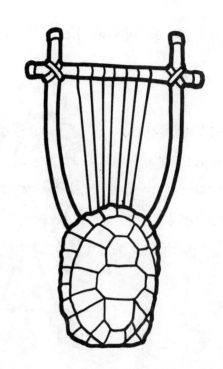

He was the son of Zeus and Leto. He was the twin brother of Artemis. He was the god of archery, agriculture, poetry, music, healing, medicine, and other things. He was the most beautiful of the gods.

Artemis

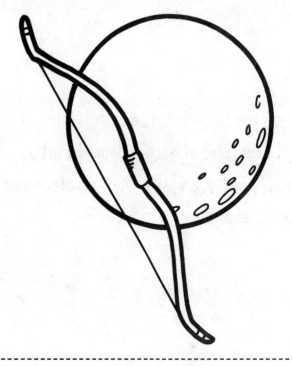

She was the daughter of Zeus and Leto and the twin sister of Apollo. She was the goddess of the moon and the hunt. She protected the young of animals and humans.

My Book of Greek Mythology *(cont.)*

Ares

He was the son of Zeus and Hera. He was the god of war.

Athena

She was the daughter of Zeus and Metis. She was the goddess of war, wisdom, the arts, justice, industry, and skill. She invented sailing ships and chariots.

My Book of Greek Mythology *(cont.)*

Aphrodite

She was the daughter of Uranus. She is called the goddess of love and beauty. She was born by rising out of the foam of the sea. She was married to Hephaestus, the lame, smith-god.

Hephaestus

He was the god of volcanoes. He was an artist in metal-working. He created armor for the gods and heroes. He made thunderbolts for Zeus. He was lame and ugly, but he made beautiful things, and he was kind.

My Book of Greek Mythology *(cont.)*

Demeter

She was the goddess of fruitfulness and grain.
She created winter when her daughter
Persephone was kidnapped by Hades.

Persephone

She was the daughter of Zeus and Demeter.
She was the wife of Hades. When she was in
the underworld, it was winter and fall. When
she was in the upper world, it was spring
and summer.

146

My Book of Greek Mythology (cont.)

Hermes

Hermes was the god of trade, travel, hunting, and exploring. He was the messenger of the gods and the protector of travelers, merchants, and thieves. He was a very tricky god.

Eros

He was the son of Aphrodite. He was the god of love and power. He did not get older, but he did get younger! He traveled around spreading love with his arrow.

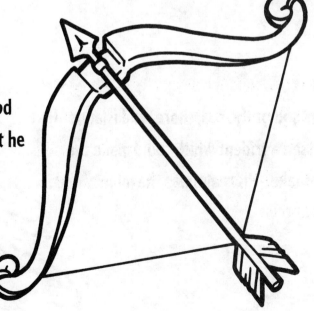

My Book of Greek Mythology (cont.)

Hades

He was the god of the underworld.
The underworld was not a bad place in Greek
mythology; it was where all of the dead people
went. To get to Hades, the soul crossed the
river Styx on a ferry boat.

Poseidon

He was god of the sea, shore, and islands. He
possessed a trident which could make the
earth shake. His realm was the mighty ocean.

My Book of Greek Mythology *(cont.)*

Dionysus

The youngest of the gods, Dionysus was the god of wine, vegetation, fertility, and the dramatic arts. He was a son of Zeus. Humans who disobeyed Dionysus were struck mad.

Selene

She is the moon. She comes out at night to light up the world while her brother the sun is asleep. She drives milk-white horses across the sky at night. Her light is the magical light of the moon.

My Book of Greek Mythology *(cont.)*

Prometheus

He was a Titan who was in charge of bringing people to the world. He felt sorry for people and wanted to give them fire. Zeus said no, but Prometheus was a rebel against authority and brought fire to the human race in spite of Zeus.

Pandora

She was the first woman. She was given a box by Zeus and told not to open it. She became curious and opened the box, releasing the evils of the world. She managed to keep Hope for the world.

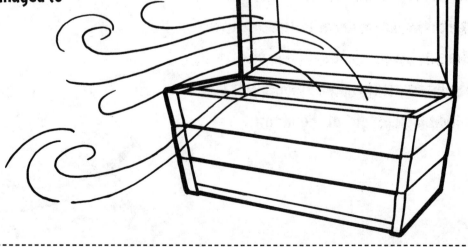

My Book of Greek Mythology *(cont.)*

Eos

She was the goddess of the dawn. She was also the mother of four winds: Boreas, Zephyrus, Notus, and Eurus.

Helios

He was the god of the sun. He reported the activities on earth to the other gods. He rode across the sky in a golden chariot. At night he rode under the world on a golden boat.

My Book of Greek Mythology *(cont.)*

Orpheus

He was the son of Calliope and the best musician the world ever knew. He played the lyre and the animals would follow him just to hear his music.

Herakles

He was a half-god and hero. He was the son of Zeus and Alcmene. He was famous for many amazing feats and the Twelve Labors of Herakles. He is also known as Hercules.

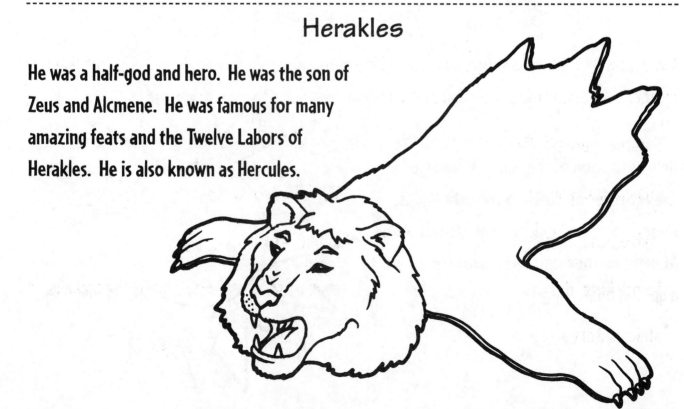

My Book of Greek Mythology *(cont.)*

Mnemosyne

She was the goddess of memory and mother of the muses.

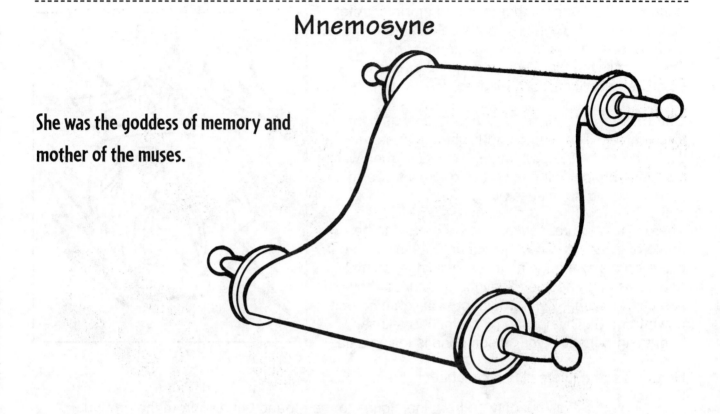

The Muses

The muses were the daughters of Zeus and Mnemosyne. They turned the stories that their mother told them into poems and music so that they would not be forgotten.

Euterpe, flute playing

Thaleia, comedy

Melpomene, tragedy

Terpsichore, dance

Kleio, history

Erato, love poems

Polymnia, sacred music

Ourania, astrology

Kalliope, epic poetry (She holds the highest rank of the Muses.)

The Thunder and Lightning of Zeus

Zeus was the father of the gods and mortals. After he and the other Olympian gods defeated the Titans, Zeus was in charge of Olympus and Earth. The Greeks believed that Zeus and the other gods controlled every part of their lives.

One of the many things Zeus had to do was control the weather. The thunder and lightning of storms was the result of Zeus's anger. He was armed with a mighty thunderbolt that he could throw to Earth if something did not please him.

There was good reason for ancient people to be afraid of lightning. They did not understand where it came from and it often hit trees, buildings, animals, and sometimes people. They thought that if they did something wrong, Zeus would throw a lightning bolt down from Mt. Olympus to hit them. We still say, "Lightning will strike you," if someone is telling a lie.

Here are some interesting facts about lightning:

- Lightning does not only go from the clouds to the ground but also from the ground to the clouds!

- The lightning traveling from the cloud to the ground travels about 240 miles (386 km) per second. It takes about 5/1,000 of a second to make it from the clouds to the earth.

- Lightning going up travels even faster. It moves at 61,000 miles (98,170 km) per second and can make the journey in 1/10,000 of a second.

- The electrical energy in a bolt of lightning can provide enough power to lift a 2,000 lbs. (907 kg) car 62 miles (98 km) high!

- One man was hit by lightning on seven different occasions throughout his life!

The Wisdom of Athena

Athena was the goddess of wisdom. She helped people to understand the world around them. She helped philosophers and everyday people learn and understand new things.

Here is a puzzle to test the wisdom of Athena.

Unscramble the letters in each word, then unscramble the words to make sentences about the goddess Athena.

1. dowmis hatnea fo dogdses swa het

   _____

2. het hitocra psshi ahtnae nda liasngi vitnende

   _____

3. teh repants fo reew ahenat temis nad uesz

   _____

4. no vlide tmnou tenhaa ymplous

   _____

5. hcidl vofaiter uesz thenaa fo het saw

   _____

- -

Hint: Fold this section under before reproducing.

Answers: 1. Athena was the goddess of wisdom. **2.** Athena invented the chariot and sailing ships. **3.** The parents of Athena were Zeus and Metis. **4.** Athena lived on Mount Olympus. **5.** Athena was the favorite child of Zeus.

Athena and Arachne

Athena was the goddess of wisdom. She taught man how to use tools and helped him to invent the ax, the plough, the yoke, the wheel, and the sail. She was also the goddess who invented the loom and weaving.

She was very proud of her skill as a weaver. As a young girl she wove a bed cover for her father, Zeus, that was woven from the clouds around Mount Olympus. It was dyed the colors of the sunset.

On Earth a young girl named Arachne was the most talented weaver among humans. She wove the finest garments and capes that the kings admired. She was famous for her skill, and she became very proud.

Arachne was so sure of her skill as a weaver that she boasted to the people in her land that she was better than Athena. What Arachne did not realize was that the gods listened to the conversations of the humans, and the gods were very jealous.

Athena was angry about Arachne's boastfulness. She came to Earth and knocked on Arachne's door. She challenged Arachne to a weaving contest, and Arachne had no choice but to go along with the idea.

The two women wove their best. Arachne wove a tapestry of fine threads, and she wove into it stories of the people who lived on the earth. When she held up her work, the people applauded and praised her.

Athena then went to work. Athena used the clouds to weave a perfect tapestry. She wove scenes from Mount Olympus that no mortal person could ever hope to see. When Athena was done, the people cried at the beauty of it.

Even though Athena won the contest, she still punished Arachne. She told Arachne that if she wanted to spin and weave, she could do so for all time. The goddess then turned Arachne into a spider on a web.

This is why spiders are called "arachnids" today.

Arachne Puppet Pattern

Materials

- scissors
- tagboard or lightweight cardboard
- 8 long pipe cleaners for each spider
- glue
- crayons or markers

Directions

1. Use the pattern on the next page to create an Arachne spider.

2. Trace the pattern on tagboard or another lightweight board.

3. Color the spider in Greek-style designs. Use bright colors.

4. Punch four holes along each side of the spider.

5. Put a pipe cleaner leg in each hole. Twist to keep in place.

6. Attach the holding strip on the back of the spider with glue or tape. The holding strip should be bent enough that you can get your finger behind the strip to hold on to the spider.

7. Hook the holding strip with your finger and make your spider dance.

8. Act out the story of Arachne and Athena with your spider.

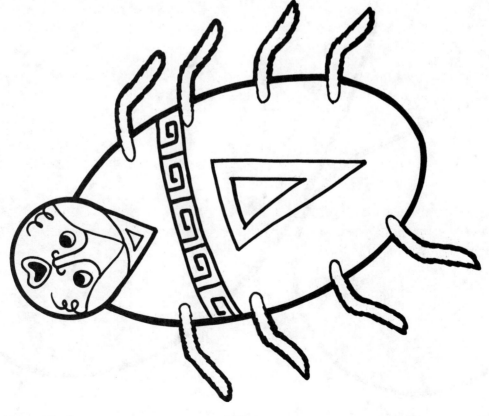

Arachne Puppet Pattern *(cont.)*

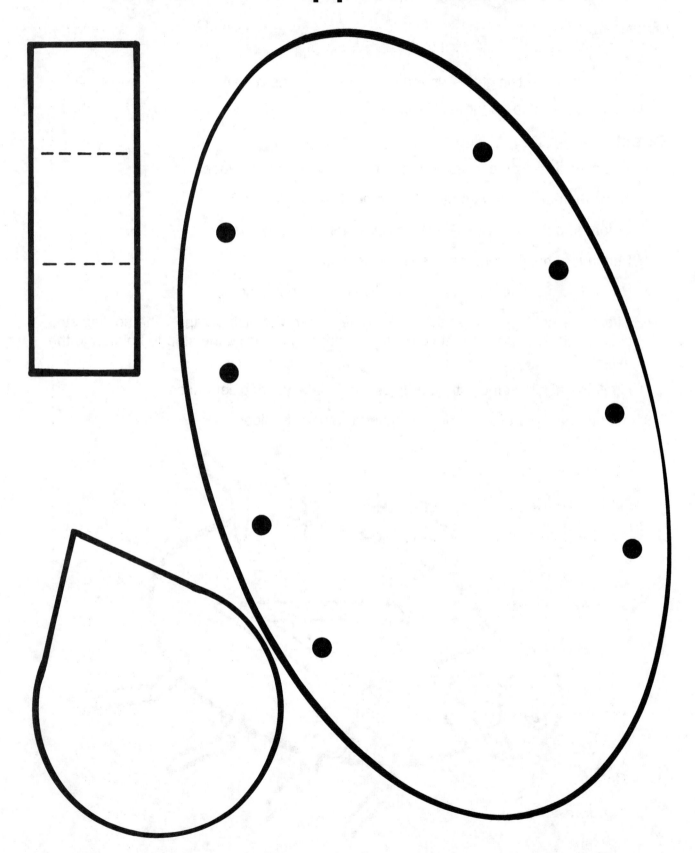

Hunting for the Gods

Artemis was the goddess of the hunt. She protected young animals and people. Help her hunt for the names of the gods in this search puzzle.

```
A  R  O  D  N  A  P  C  M  A  V  A  I  P  B
V  I  Z  H  M  R  Q  M  R  U  R  O  F  A  P
T  S  P  X  Y  A  E  E  A  T  H  L  K  W  X
S  C  G  Q  N  F  S  T  E  Q  Q  L  T  I  J
N  E  R  E  J  T  L  M  E  J  F  O  S  I  P
A  P  H  R  O  D  I  T  E  M  G  P  T  P  Y
S  T  X  Y  H  S  I  A  R  A  E  A  X  O  K
A  H  E  R  M  E  S  O  K  M  R  D  W  S  H
R  L  Y  W  S  U  L  F  N  S  U  E  Z  E  A
T  M  H  B  O  P  Y  I  R  Y  K  Z  H  I  D
S  D  A  O  R  A  A  P  O  V  S  H  U  D  E
Y  E  M  P  E  O  N  V  R  S  N  U  N  O  S
S  Q  S  V  K  B  I  M  C  G  I  G  S  N  U
```

Aphrodite	**Apollo**	**Ares**
Artemis	**Athena**	**Demeter**
Dionysus	**Eros**	**Hades**
Helios	**Hera**	**Hermes**
Pandora	**Poseidon**	**Zeus**

Hunting for the Gods Answer Key

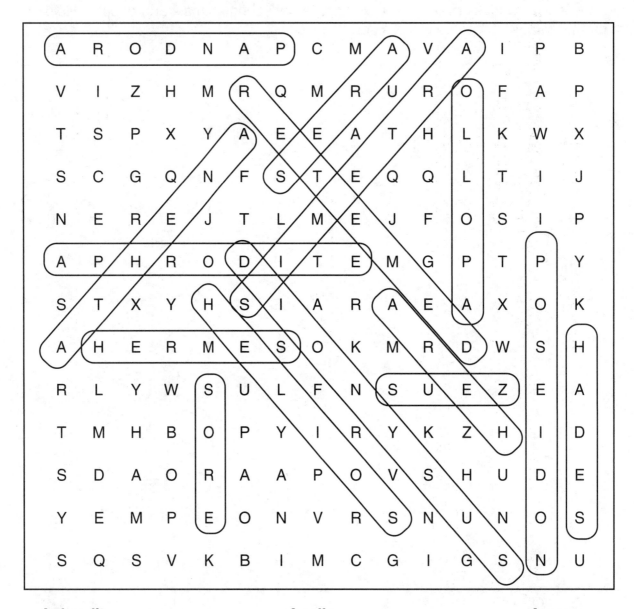

Aphrodite   **Apollo**   **Ares**

Artemis   **Athena**   **Demeter**

Dionysus   **Eros**   **Hades**

Helios   **Hera**   **Hermes**

Pandora   **Poseidon**   **Zeus**

The A-mazing Feats of Theseus

Theseus was a great hero of Greek mythology. He did many brave things in his lifetime. He cleared the roads of Athens of robbers and bandits. He fought strange monsters and often proved his strength and bravery. But his biggest test was defeating the Minotaur.

The Minotaur was a very large and dangerous beast. It lived in a cave that was full of twisted passageways. Once someone went into the cave, it would be almost impossible to find a way out. The cave twisted and turned like a great maze, and it was called the "Labyrinth of Crete."

Every nine years the king of Crete would throw seven young men and seven young women into the Labyrinth. They would become lost and unable to find their way out. Then the Minotaur would find them and eat them. The king did this because his son was killed accidentally at the annual sporting games, and he was bitter about his son's death.

Theseus heard about the horrible Minotaur. He went to Crete to try to kill the monster.

The daughter of the king of Crete helped Theseus. Her name was Ariadne. She gave Theseus a string of gold and told him to unwind it as he entered the Labyrinth. After he found and killed the Minotaur, he would be able to find his way out of the maze by following the gold thread.

The plan worked. Theseus carefully left the gold thread behind him as he made his way through the passages of the cave. He found the Minotaur and killed him with his powerful sword. Then he took the head of the Minotaur and followed the string to safety.

He and Ariadne ran away from the island of Crete to return to Athens.

The A-mazing Feats of Theseus *(cont.)*

You need to help Theseus find the Minotaur. Trace a path through this maze. Begin at "Start" and find the Minotaur. Be sure to leave a trail that will help you find your way out again!

Here is your maze.

START

162

The A-mazing Feats of Theseus Maze Answer Key

START

Helping You Remember

Mnemosyne was the goddess of memory. We use her name today when we use "mnemonics" or tricks to help us remember things. Mnemonics can be very helpful to you in remembering new things.

Here are some examples:

If you want to remember all of the names of the Great Lakes, just think of "homes." Each letter in "homes" is the first letter of one of the lakes: Huron, Ontario, Michigan, Erie, Superior. This might not help you learn about the lakes, but it will help you remember their names.

Remembering the order of the planets from the sun might be easier if you remember this sentence: "My very eager mother just served us nine pizzas." There are nine planets and nine words in the sentence. The sentence also mentions the number nine. Each word in the sentence begins with the same letter as a planet. Mercury, Venus, Earth, Mars, Jupiter, Saturn, Uranus, Neptune, Pluto. This is the order of the planets from the sun.

Another mnemonic helps us remember the colors of the rainbow. If you think of a guy named Roy G. Biv, you will be able to think of the colors of the rainbow in their proper order. Can you guess the colors that the letters stand for?

R _____   O _____   Y _____   G _____

B _____   I _____   V _____

Can you think of any other mnemonics? If you do, share them with your classmates. Maybe you will help them with their memory!

Hint: Fold this section under before reproducing.

Answers: red, orange, yellow, green, blue, indigo, violet

A Mischievous God

Hermes was the messenger of the gods. He was very playful and mischievous, but all of the gods of Olympus found him to be clever and amusing. Zeus enjoyed Hermes' company so much that he gave him the job of being the messenger of the gods.

Hermes was a very good messenger because he could travel very quickly. He could get around fast because he had a hat and sandals with wings on them. Because he was such a clever and quick messenger, Zeus let him have several jobs on Mount Olympus. Hermes became the patron of thieves, gamblers, and shepherds. He also protected travelers and helped to guide souls to the underworld. He was the god of commerce.

Hermes was very clever and invented many things in his workshop on Mount Olympus. He was the inventor of the alphabet, playing cards, card games, the lyre, and the reed flute.

When the Romans adopted the Greek gods, they gave Hermes the name of Mercury. Mercury is also the name of the planet that is closest to the sun. The planet Mercury is the fastest of the planets in our solar system.

Mercury is also the name of one of the elements on the periodic chart of the elements. Mercury is a liquid, but it looks like runny silver. When mercury is dropped, it "breaks" into tiny balls and rolls very quickly all over the place. When the balls touch each other, they form into a larger blob. Mercury is fun to watch, but it is dangerous to touch.

On the next page is a pattern to make a set of wings. Color and cut out the wings. You might want to glue the wings onto stiffer paper. Attach them to a pair of sandals or to a hat. Ask your teacher if you can be the class messenger.

Interesting Fact: Sandals with wings are called *talaria*.

The Wings of Hermes

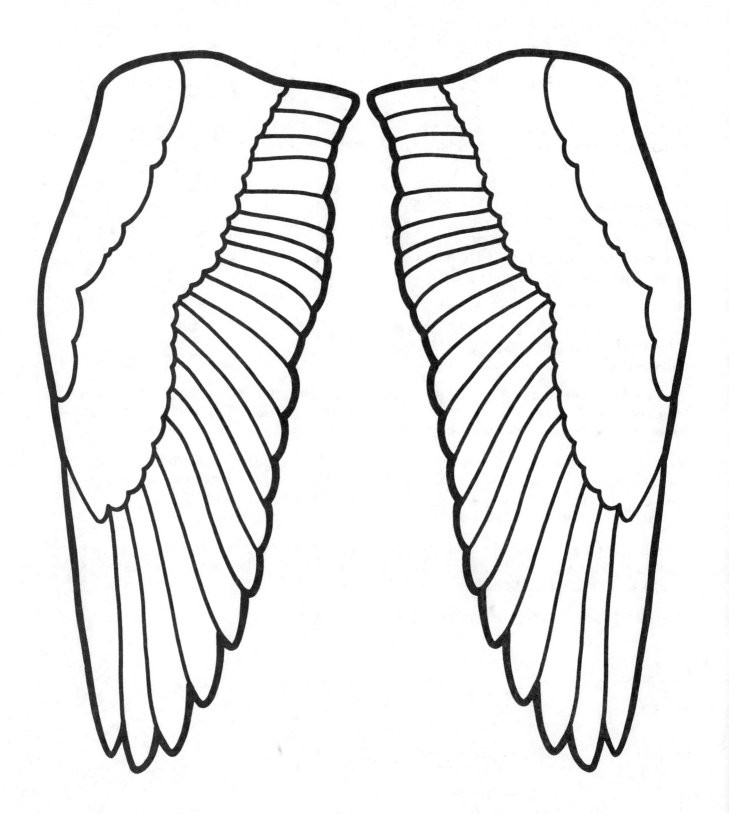

The Lyre

The ancient Greeks loved music. In fact, music is an important part of Greek life even today.

One instrument invented by the Greeks was the lyre. This stringed instrument was said to have been invented by the mischievous god, Hermes. Hermes made the first lyre from the shell of a turtle. He gave the lyre to his half-brother Apollo in exchange for his cattle.

Apollo loved to play the lyre and his music was magical. He was the god of music and his voice could be heard singing from Mt. Olympus.

If you would like to make a lyre, directions are in *A Civilization Project Book for Ancient Greece* by Susan Purdy and Cass R. Sandak.

Enhance your knowledge about Greek music and learn more about other Greek instruments by using reference sources such as encyclopedias, books about Greek music, and the Internet.

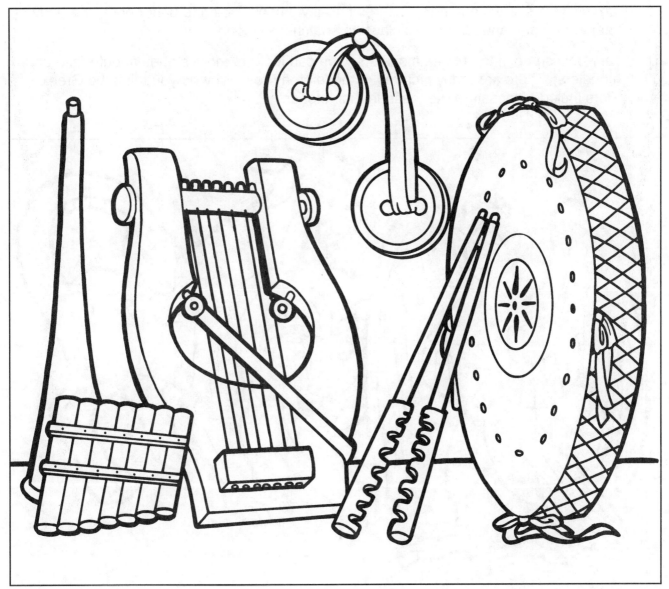

Greek Monsters

The Greek myths are full of unusual monsters. The *centaurs* are half man and half horse. The *chimera* had the head of a lion, the body of a goat, and the tail of a serpent. *Cerberus* was the hound of Hades and was said to have three to fifty heads.

Echidna was a horrible monster that was half serpent and half woman. She was the mother of other horrible monsters which included *Cerberus, Hydra, Ladon, Chimera, Sphinx,* and *Nemean Lion*.

Medusa was one of the *Gorgons*. On her head, she had snakes instead of hair. When people looked at her face, they were immediately turned to stone. She was finally defeated by Perseus who killed her as he looked at her reflection in a mirror.

The *Minotaur* was half man and half bull. He lived in a cave that was a huge maze. No one could get out of it until Ariadne told Theseus how to escape.

The *Harpies* were scary creatures. A Harpy had a woman's face and upper body, the body of a bird, ears of a bear, and long sharp claws to snatch away food.

These are only some of the Greek monsters. You can look up more stories about these and other monsters. There are many pictures of these creatures. Why do you think the Greek storytellers included monsters like these in their stories?

168

Design Your Own Mythical Beast

The Greek storytellers created monsters by combining parts of people and animals. You can create your own monster by doing the same thing. Cut out the pictures below and on page 170 and create your own monster. Write a story to go along with your creature. Is your creation going to be bad or good?

Design Your Own Mythical Beast *(cont.)*

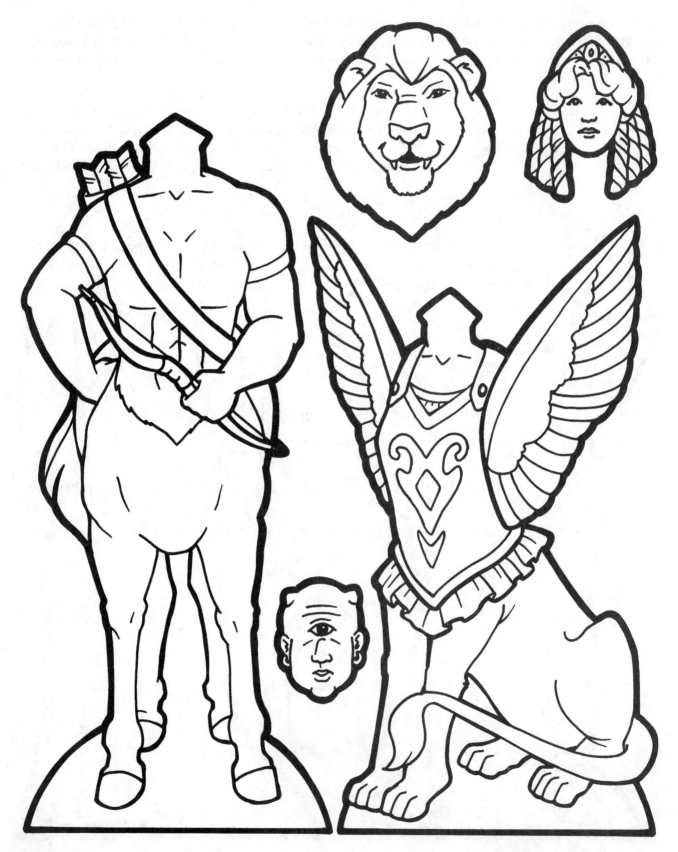

Aesop's Fables

Have your students heard about the tortoise and the hare? How about the dog in the manger? Do they know about the grasshopper that played all summer while the ant worked? These stories are all ones that are said to have been written by a man named Aesop. They have become an important part of our culture.

It is generally believed that Aesop was a slave and lived from 620 to 565 B.C. and was given his freedom as a result of his stories. The stories were called *fables* because they were used to teach a moral lesson. Most of the fables have animals as main characters and animals speak and act with emotions just like humans. Some fables deal with plants, the sea, the sun, the wind, or the Greek gods.

In about 300 B.C., a book of 200 of Aesop's fables was created by Demetrius. No one knows if he made them all up, but people enjoyed the clever tales.

Fables are wonderful to share with your class. They offer the opportunity to teach not only a literary genre, but also the chance to discuss human nature and values with the student. Reading a fable a day to your class is something that they will look forward to and learn to appreciate. Fables offer a great venue for stimulating discussions in the classroom.

Discussion Topics

- Who would laugh hardest at this story?

- Why did Aesop make up this story?

- Why was being able to tell a good story such an important gift back then?

- Compare storytelling to the types of entertainment we have today.
  (TV, CDs, radio programs, etc.)

- It is said that Aesop could make people laugh. Can you think of a famous comedian who makes you laugh?

- Have you ever had someone tell you a story? Who? Was it funny? Sad? Scary? Did it teach you something?

Aesop's Fables *(cont.)*

Across many countries there are professional storytellers who visit libraries, museums, and schools to share their stories. Many stories are handed down from one generation to the next. They even have get-togethers where you can buy a ticket and have a whole day of hearing wonderful, imaginative stories.

You can find hundreds more stories online at *www.aesopfables.com*

Software, like Danny Glover's *Aesop's Fables*, includes the stories with illustrations, mazes, and puzzles.

After the students have become familiar with the fables and have heard a variety of them, have them try to write a fable of their own. Use the next page to help them get started. Discuss the use of animals in human roles. Stress the importance of teaching a lesson at the end of the story. Explain that fables have to be short and straight to the point. Fables usually have only two characters. Discuss the meanings of the characteristics of various characters in the fables. Have the students draw pictures to accompany their fables. Read them aloud to the class.

Use these morals as ideas:

- Not everything you see is what it appears to be.

- Do not attempt to hide things that cannot be hidden.

- Enemies make promises that are meant to be broken.

- Liars do not keep their friends long.

- Helping others helps yourself.

- Sometimes you win when you seem to lose.

Create a Fable

Fable Title: _____

My Name (Author): _____

Describe who your characters will be and write about their characteristics.

Character #1: _____

_____

Character #2: _____

_____

Character #3 (optional): _____

_____

Character #4 (optional): _____

_____

Setting: _____

_____

_____

_____

_____

_____

_____

_____

Create a Fable *(cont.)*

Write your fable here.

_____
_____
_____
_____
_____
_____
_____
_____
_____
_____
_____
_____
_____
_____
_____

The moral of my fable is: _____

Citizen of the World Award

This award is presented to

_____

for completing our study of Greece

A good citizen displays . . .

- helpfulness to others
- good study habits
- a good attitude in the classroom

_____ _____

date teacher's signature

It's Not All Greek to Me Anymore!

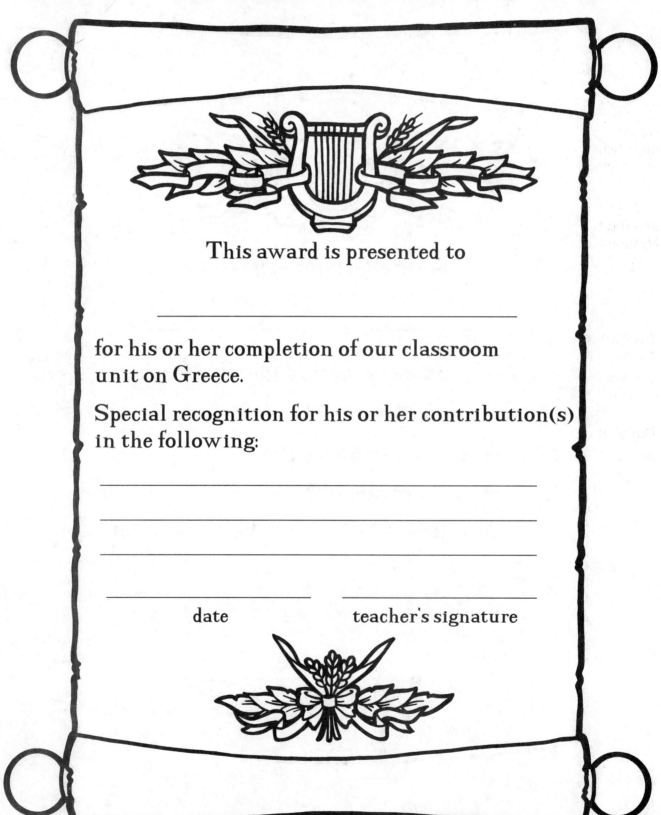

This award is presented to

_____

for his or her completion of our classroom
unit on Greece.

Special recognition for his or her contribution(s)
in the following:

_____

_____

_____

_____   _____
date   teacher's signature